Artilleryman

Richard,
The only way to
have a friend is to
be one!

John

Artilleryman

A Memoir of World War II

By
John T. Varano

To order additional copies of this book, contact:
Xlibris Corporation
1-888-795-4274
www.Xlibris.com
Orders@Xlibris.com
74200

Contents

Acknowledgments

Special thanks must go out to my dear friend, Diane Larson, whose tireless effort made this book possible. Her assistance was invaluable, from the first to the final word of the manuscript. While visiting one afternoon with her children, she saw my disconnected notes and jottings spread out on the dining room table and asked what I was doing. Sheepishly, I told her I was trying to write my war story. She saw my obvious lack of organizational skills and offered her help. With a degree in English and a talent for the written word, she went to work. She volunteered her time, listened to my adventures and misadventures, wrote it down, researched, read it aloud for me, revised, and started the process over again with each new chapter. Diane was indispensable in helping me to write my story. Her labor was selfless and I can never thank her enough. Without her expertise, questions, and persistence, this book never would have been written. I am forever grateful.

A heart felt thank you goes to my niece, Sharman Rodriguez. Sharman donated countless hours of her personal time and talent editing and proofing the draft of my memoirs before it went to print. To my daughters, Mary, Norma, and Toni, thank you for your endless energy, enthusiasm, and love that went into preparing the final draft for publishing.

Introduction

My story covers almost three years of my life when I was an artilleryman in the European Theater. The news of the day was so important and ghastly, so far-reaching and complex, so uncommon and courageous, that there can never be enough history books written to describe and explain the events of WWII. This is a personal history, however, and I was a young soldier, one who wrote letters and kept journals and planned to write about it. But then, after the war, it became too difficult, and I rarely even spoke of it.

Half a century later, as a father, husband, and grandfather, I finally retired from running my own business, and realized now I had the time and must use it. With books, maps, and random notes scattered around me, I proved to be a most disorganized writer. One evening, in the midst of the media coverage of the 50th Anniversary of World War II, my daughter, Norma, called me. She was crying. She had just watched a television documentary about the war and it included footage of my Division, the 90th Infantry, Patton's Third Army.

Norma was shocked to see even a little of what I had gone through. She wanted to know more and encouraged me to write it down. My son, John, a soldier in the Bosnian Conflict, wanted to read my story. My daughters, Mary and Toni, supported my efforts. And I wanted my children and grandchildren to know what it was like for me as a young man and how I survived in Europe during World War II.

It took six years to write my story, during which time I relied on the patience and strength of my wife, Victoria. My obsessive determination to write this memoir baffled her at times, but she was always there for me, the love of my life, my best friend, and my soul mate. My gratitude to her is limitless.

Man is an adaptable being, I've come to believe. After the war, I could put aside the guns and the horror and not speak of it. As I got older, I wanted to speak of it, and this is for anyone who wants to listen.

Chapter One

Drafted

The Army drafted me in August 1943. In one month, I would turn 19 and in four months I would have graduated from high school and trade school. I had dual enrollment. Raised Catholic in an Italian-American family, I was the eldest boy of four children. My mother went to Mass and prayed the rosary every day. Mama cried when I got my draft notice. She was devastated. My father took the news silently, but sadness, like a shadow, fell across his usually stoic face. Papa had fought in the Italian Army in WW1 and walked with a limp from the shrapnel still embedded in his leg. He was a great speaker and fired my imagination when he described the battles he'd fought in Albania. A self-educated man, he taught me history and current events. Every week he bought the Italian Progressive Paper and kept abreast of activities in Europe. We spoke Italian at home and English outside the home.

We lived in a green and white one-story house at the bottom of a hill in New Britain, Connecticut. The morning I left for basic training, I avoided my mother's face. She looked like someone had died. Sorrow filled the house. She cooked my breakfast, set my place at the table and would have fed me if I had allowed it.

"Don't go, Johnny," she begged.

My father tried to console her, "Grace, it is God's will."

"We carry our sons in our womb, raise them with love, teach them to be children of God. Then we send them to war to be killed? This is not God's will!" She began to cry.

It was time to drive me to the train station. I didn't think she could get more distraught, but when we walked out on the open front porch, she embraced me and wouldn't let go, crying, pleading. Relatives who had come to see me off had to pry Mama off me. I blew her a kiss as we drove away, "Don't worry Mama, I'll come back, I promise."

Papa, my sisters, Florence and Josephine, and my little brother, Vinny said goodbye from the platform at the train station. I waved through the open window and saw tears streaming down my father's face. It was the second time I'd seen him cry. The first time was during the depression when he'd lost his job.

I wanted to go. I was ready. I had big plans. I was going to be an Army Air Force pilot. I tried to enlist on the day I registered for the draft, at City Hall, the first business day after my 18th birthday. I didn't tell Mama. The clerk in charge at the Draft Board told me to come back when I was a certified mechanic, a skill that was essential in wartime. I kept trying to enlist and she got sick of my face. "Not you again."

I wanted to stop the Nazis, and I wanted to fly airplanes. To me, Hitler was evil incarnate. He had taken over Europe and overpowered Italy where my parents were born and where I'd spent a wonderful year of my childhood. I wanted to be a fighter pilot in the Army Air Force. I always wanted to fly, but I could not afford aviation school in nearby Putnam. When I was growing up, airplanes flying overhead were a big deal. I made and collected model airplanes. The neighborhood boys and I played with light balsam gliders until they splintered. Everything stopped when we heard the drone of a propeller engine. We'd run out and look to the sky as the sound got louder and closer. I was going to fly. I'd enrolled in trade school to learn combustible engines, the closest I could get to airplane engines. Dominic, my paisan, was a pilot. His father and my mother came from the same town in Italy, Santa Catarina. Dominic lived in my neighborhood, graduated eight years before me, and was a Colonel in the Army Air Force. I idolized him even after his plane crashed and he lost an eye in a freak landing accident. He couldn't fly anymore, but the Army assigned him to experiment with new aircraft engines—top secret. He had guards on him twenty-four hours a day but managed to smuggle manuals to me so I could study the latest schematics on military aircraft engines.

We unloaded from the train at Fort Devens, Massachusetts. I took aptitude tests, oral and written exams, on aviation and aircraft mechanics. I was tested in a simulator, where I released bombs on imaginary targets. Two days later, in the late afternoon, I was put on a train, destination unknown. That's how it was in the Army, everything kept secret. You didn't know where you were going until you got there.

I arrived at Fort Bragg, North Carolina and wondered why was I at the largest Artillery Base in the United States? Never had I planned to be in the Artillery. Sure, I'd played with guns. My father had a revolver that he kept unloaded in his top dresser drawer. I played with it when no one was home. I'd gone pheasant hunting with Tony Morelli and his father when I was 11 or 12, and I had a squirt gun and a B.B. gun, but that was it.

The course lasted 17 weeks. I learned to be a cannoneer, part of a seven-man gun crew for the 105 MM Howitzer, direct support to infantry. Midway through the training period, I was summoned to military headquarters. I reported to the Warrant Officer, the one in charge of paperwork.

"Private Varano reporting as requested sir."

"At ease, Private, sit down please. I know you are curious to know why you are at Fort Bragg." He thumbed through the papers in his hand, which I presumed were about me.

"You did very well on the written exams, even up against college men. But I have bad news Private. You didn't make it."

"Sir?" I sat bolt upright in my chair, in disbelief.

"You flunked the eye coordination test. You missed the target every time."

The officer showed me the dots on a paper that represented where my bombs fell during the simulation, always off the mark.

"Consider yourself lucky, Private. Because of your training, you're in the artillery instead of the infantry."

My only thought was 'shoot me now and get it over with' as I walked out of the building and looked for a place to hide. I crawled into the first boiler room I could find, under an Army barracks, and slumped to the floor. I wept like a child. I came out of the boiler room and didn't tell anyone. The intensity of basic training kept me occupied, kept me moving. We were out in the heat most of the time, 90-100 degrees. We practically lived in the field and there was no shade. Some days we were woken up at 0100 hours for what seemed like an endless march order. An easier day saw us up at 0500 hours; an hour of calisthenics before breakfast, then we crawled on our bellies out in the field, slogged through the mud, or scaled walls. I had trouble with one of the obstacles on the course. I had to swing across a large, muddy expanse of water with only a running start and a rope to hold onto. I fell in the muddy water, again and again. The Sergeant in charge said, "Listen you little goddamn son of a bitch, get your sorry ass up and over that stream. Where do you think you are, at home, with your mother, putting diapers on you? Don't you know how to handle a rope? I'm telling you right now, Private Varano, you little piece of shit, you're going to cross that stream, if it takes all night."

It looked like it might, I just couldn't get up the momentum, I was getting more tired by the minute. I had rope burns and wasn't used to that kind of abusive language. Finally, my buddies distracted the Sergeant and one of the big strong guys told me, "Hold on." He grabbed me by the legs, pulled me back as far as he could, and gave me a strong push on the backside. I flew over that stream like Tarzan and let go of the rope as soon as I saw dry earth on the other side, dropping to the ground with a hard thud.

I was a teenager, first time away from home. Basic training turned me into a soldier. From boy to man in 17 weeks, a near impossible task, but I completed basic training and was changed for good.

It helped to have good teachers, quality officers that ran the Artillery School. They taught me how to stay alive, work as a team, fire the big gun, and kill or be killed.

Next stop, Fort Mead, Maryland, where I was processed and reassigned as a replacement. I was there for a month; long enough to have all my buddies from Fort Bragg reassigned to other replacement camps. All I saw were unfamiliar faces. I was now in 'advanced' training with hand to hand combat and weaponry. I was shot at with live ammunition.

I had a four-day pass and went home to say goodbye. There was a big, impromptu party. All the relatives and friends showed up and brought my favorite foods in covered dishes. The word spread, "Johnny's home, let's go say goodbye."

Mama made spaghetti, pizza, and lasagna. The wine flowed, homemade Italian wine that my father made and for which he was known throughout the neighborhood. Everyone told me I looked good in uniform. I'd survived basic training, and I was solid and strong. The morning I left, it was like all the party balloons burst at once. Mama cried, but she was resigned and she let me go.

We embarked from Camp Shank in New York. I boarded a Navy transport ship in the middle of the night. It was February, bitter cold, a sky full of stars. We had a 35-pound field artillery pack on our backs and carried a duffel bag with all the gear we'd use in our life as soldiers. The Salvation Army was there, handing out coffee and donuts as we stepped onto the gangplank, and a small Army band played, a little warmth and light in a cold dark night.

The hull of the ship was huge; our sleeping quarters were in the center, bunks like hammocks, one on top of the other. Someone said there were 1200 men on board. By 0400 hours, we were asleep in our hammocks and out in open seas. I was rudely awakened by rough weather, the ship felt like a toy boat tossed around in a bathtub. I got seasick, and once the vomiting began, it started from the top hammock and moved down. The smell alone was nauseating. I yelled at the guy above me, "Hey, you just puked on my head!" and then I lost it, leaned over and threw up on the guy below me. It seemed that the vomiting would never stop.

The storms and high seas continued throughout the Atlantic crossing. Our transport ship was part of a navy convoy that included destroyers. We were somewhere out in the middle of the Atlantic when the sirens went off. Our escort had spotted a German submarine. We employed evasive maneuvers that took us as far north as Iceland.

The Army was not evasive when it came to regular immunization against disease. Soldiers were vaccinated according to a strict timetable. We were due for our shots during the Atlantic crossing. One morning our Sergeant yelled out, "Get naked from the waist up and get your ass up on top deck." A roar of protest went up, but we obeyed orders. It was zero degrees up there and windy too. We huddled against each other. I was freezing. My teeth chattered. We felt like prisoners of war, naked to the elements, lined up for torture. The ship rocked in the high seas. We moved in single file from top deck, down to the bottom of the hull, to the infirmary. A team of doctors and medics had set up tables. The ship rolled and the doctors gave injections. Often, a needle broke off in the soldier's arm, only to be removed with a hemostat and the injection given again. Men's screams echoed through the bottom hull of the ship, but we got our shots right on time. I got only one injection and didn't feel that one. I was so cold I was blue.

We disembarked in Barry, Wales. Once again, it was the dead of night. We loaded into trucks and were transported to our new camp. It felt strange to be on solid ground. Camp was a golf course that overlooked the town of Barry. It had been converted into an ammunition depot. That night, we ate some sort of soup, more accurately "slop." We had coffee and bread with marmalade. To this day I cannot eat marmalade.

We stowed our gear in tents where we would live for the next three months. When assigning guard duty, those in command chose to start with the end of the alphabet, so Varano was on guard duty the first night in Wales. We did not yet have our regular Army issue carbines, a 30-caliber rifle. They hadn't made it off the ship yet. We assembled as ordered in a room for the guards, and I could not believe my eyes when we were issued World War I vintage Springfield rifles. The Springfield was a good weapon, but each time it was fired, you had to pull back the bolt to reload. The gun was twice as heavy as the carbine I was used to, and boy did it pack a powerful kick.

We marched to our designated posts for guard duty that night. The Corporal of the guard said, "Fire one shot in the air to signal an emergency."

It was so dark at times I could not see my hand in front of my eyes. It was windy and rainy and occasionally the moon broke through the clouds to reveal bare trees blowing back and forth. Wind through the leafless branches made an eerie sound, like someone prowling through the area. Half way through my first round of guard duty, the Corporal came to warn me, "Hey, Varano, they're dropping German parachutes in this area. Watch your ass."

Not even ten minutes passed and I heard the distant drone of airplanes from the direction of the coast. I was guarding ammunition stockpiles. I couldn't see any of the other guards. Blackness surrounded me and the moving trees made the weirdest sound. I did not know what the terrain looked like, never having seen it in daylight. I pushed my back up against a tree.

The wind gusted, strongly and noisily. I swung around and fired at something behind me, a sound I had never heard before.

All the guards came running. I had sounded the alarm. A group of German parachutists were captured in our vicinity, so my potential reprimand for shooting at ghosts turned into a commendation. I had alerted the company, and enemy soldiers were taken prisoner.

After four hours, my relief showed up. I headed back to the guardhouse and had to walk through camp. All around, men were squatting with their pants down, toilet paper streaming behind them. Soldiers were moaning, doubled over from stomach pain. The smell was unbearable. Many GI's found themselves in the field hospital the next morning. The diarrhea was traced to a large brown bar of GI issue soap that had made its way into one of the soup cauldrons. I'm glad I didn't eat that soup. Mine was bad enough.

Four months of Army life in the British Isles meant we marched all the time, interrupted only by combat training.

We covered the islands on foot. Long forced marches, 15 miles with a 35-pound pack on our backs, day and night we trudged through the fields and on the dirt roads in GI issue 100% English wool socks.

"These socks are the only thing keeping my feet from falling off," I said. My feet were numb; I was sore, sleep-deprived, and weather-beaten. I hated the wool; it itched and made me hot, but I was glad for the protection. The wool was a barrier that kept the sweat and dirt off my feet.

One good thing about forced hikes through the rolling countryside—we couldn't help but notice that Wales was a beautiful island. One night we were off duty and went into Barry to see a movie, "Lost Horizon." Another time we went to an amusement park. There was a Ferris wheel, merry-go-round, bumper cars, and a boat ride. I ate fish and chips and drank warm soda pop while some guys chugged down warm beer. I didn't start drinking beer until the war was over and I was stationed in Germany. At the amusement park, civilians and soldiers mixed. A handful of guys went out with Welsh girls, but who had the time or energy? I certainly didn't.

We left Wales the first of May and arrived in the village of Chard, England. May was cold and rainy, and we longed for the sunny, April weather we'd had in Wales. Chard is just south of London. Training was hell in Wales, but it got worse in England. Camp in Chard was like prison. We had no time to ourselves. The officers were cold and impersonal. We trained from dawn to dusk on good days and were often woken up in the middle of the night to march, long hikes to nowhere: sleep deprivation training. We were always hungry. We had little meat, the soup was slop, and we had hardly any bread. We lived on K rations, little round cans of cheese, spam, and biscuits. We left camp only as a company, and that was when we were given tactical problems to solve in the field. We were isolated.

Shortly after midnight on June 6, 1944, the sudden roar of planes overhead put us on alert. The reverberation filled the night and drowned out every other sound. Waves of aircraft thundered one after another in large formations, and continued into morning. D-day had begun.

At dawn we loaded onto Army transport trucks and drove to the Port of Southampton, a huge British Naval Base. Each soldier received pills to fight seasickness because the English Channel had rough weather and high seas. From there we boarded naval craft, and as we got closer to Normandy, we transferred into LCI's (landing craft infantry). The seasick pills gave us diarrhea. There was no place to go except in our pants. I'd rinse off after I was dumped into the English Channel on the French side. We headed for Utah Beach. It was late afternoon.

Chapter Two

D Day, D-Day + 1

Thirty of us were crammed shoulder to shoulder in the LCI. We were smacked up and down, battered by the waves, and things were about to get worse.

"Dump them out here. We're not going in any further. Not after the hell I went through this morning." The Officer in Charge of the LCI wanted to get the hell out of there. Shells exploded in the distance, the sea air was thick with smoke from the acrid smell of gunpowder and explosives. We heard the resonant boom of the heavy stuff coming in from the naval ships.

"Get going," the officer commanded. The ramp lowered and we were dumped into the water, no closer than 100 yards from shore. The LCI took off almost before the last man jumped out. Between the beach and us, we saw big railroad spikes sticking up. Army engineers deactivated or detonated mines attached to the spikes. The afternoon sun broke through, and rays of light filtered through the smoke and shone on the rough waves. Remnants of equipment and bits of weaponry were being washed ashore. We did not like being dumped in water over our heads. We had trained for a beach landing. Air balloons in the shape of dirigibles formed a protective circle that started at the shoreline and expanded, encompassing the area where troops were put in the water. Wire cables hung down from the air balloons. This was to discourage strafing from the enemy. Low-flying pilots in the Luftwaffe would get their planes tangled in the cables.

Fully clothed and with 35 lb. packs on our backs, 30 caliber carbines held in one hand over our heads, we fought our way toward shore. The water was deep. I could not swim. The men released from the LCI stuck together; those that could swim helped those that could not. I thrashed back and forth with my legs and sometimes, I could barely touch bottom. We bobbed up and down. The waves pushed us forward.

It was like being in the middle of a fuel spill, I swallowed the polluted salt water, coughing and sputtering. I was soon covered in black oil and garbage started to stick to me. My clothes, boots, and pack were getting heavier. I tried to keep my carbine above my head, but it was no longer dry. The roar of the big guns firing from the Navy battleships was both comforting and unnerving. The cannons fired with a thundering boom. The air hissed as the shells sailed over, a delayed thud and then a crashing explosion as they made landfall. Formations of fighter planes roared above us. The sound was nearly deafening. It had been going on intermittently since early morning, like a giant, enraged beehive, an angry roar of speed and power. That was supposed to be me up there, dropping bombs and strafing enemy targets. Instead, I was down in the water, like a half-drowned pack rat, trying to make it to the beach while the battle raged on the mainland.

As we got closer to shore, my group of soldiers separated from the action of the waves, but my buddy Willie and I managed to stay close. I bobbed up and down, pumping my legs, swallowing salt water. The dirty waves seemed to bring us in and push us out at the same time. I thought of that article in Life magazine that projected 20,000 soldiers would drown on D-day, trying to get to the beaches. The closer we got to shore, the deeper it got. It was past my chin, up to my ears, I was spitting out water and grabbing for air, weighed down, fighting the undertow. Fatigue had a hold of me. I went under.

"I'm a goner," I sputtered, and tried to yell, "Goodbye Willie." I came back up and choked out, "See you in paradise."

"Goodbye John, see you too," Willie sputtered. I'd made my peace with God, but at the same time, I pleaded, Holy Mother of God, save us, help us. I saw the face of my mother, father, sisters and brother rushing past my mind's eye, with the speed of a bullet discharged from a gun.

Suddenly, Willie and I rose up out of the water. We felt the sand beneath our boots. We waddled the rest of the way to shore and collapsed on the sand.

"Are you okay soldier?" An officer came over. I was choking and too tired to talk. I nodded.

"Let's go," the officer commanded. Willie and I managed to get up, shook off the water like a dog. We were hustled off the beach. Our boots squished with each step and we could hear sniper fire.

When we told our story of rising up out of the deep, an officer explained that heavy equipment had been unloaded earlier that day, digging out trenches near the shore.

The Germans had soldiers tied up in the trees, a combat tactic adopted from the Japanese. From that vantage point, they picked off American soldiers. Thirty-five men from my assigned group of replacement soldiers were killed on the first day.

I should try to explain what it was like to be a replacement. We came ashore on D-day without being part of a Division. We were replacements until assigned. Reinforcements would have sounded a bit less expendable, but the U.S. Army in WWII, once committed to combat, was going to keep its Divisions on the line until the war ended. A steady stream of replacements replenished the Divisions. That's what I was trained for from the outset, to replace artillerymen that wouldn't make it past the beach. I've been told that over half of the replacements were casualties themselves within three days of being put on the front line. I was with my Division until the war ended. Willie and I were both lucky. We landed in the British Isles together and stayed with each other until the end of the war.

Willie was from Minnesota; his full name was William P. Tushar. He was medium height, fair-skinned, had dark hair and brown eyes. His parents were Yugoslavian immigrants, just as my parents were Italian immigrants. Willie was a Catholic and as honest as the day was long. We met while attending mass in Barry, Wales and hooked up. From then on, we watched each other's back. When we were off-duty, we took comfort in each other's company.

We spent our first night in France in the woods and were kept on edge by sniper fire. I got an hour or two of sleep in my clammy clothes while lying on the dew covered ground, wrapped in a damp woolen blanket. I did a four-hour shift of guard duty on a 50-caliber machine-gun. The night passed. I survived D-day.

Next morning we marched to the front. We stopped to rest only after we got word that the woods had been cleared of enemy personnel. Before me, a clearing opened into a field of poppies, a swaying blanket of red that stretched as far as I could see. I knelt down in the flowers, I thought of Flanders Fields, a poem written for the dead in WWI. I thought of paper poppies we wore in our lapel on Armistice Day. I was touched by this little haven in the middle of battlefields. It was strangely quiet. All the birds and insects had been blown away by the concussion of Allied bombs. I bowed my head, clasped my hands, getting down close to the warm earth on this sunny morning in northern France. The poppies were knee high. I prayed, I pleaded, I promised. "Holy Mother of God, please don't let me die. Let me suffer, but spare my life, I promise I'll return and make a pilgrimage."

I kept my promise and in 1950, which was a holy year, I made a pilgrimage to Rome. Meanwhile, my mother, back in the states was making a similar plea in the name of the Sacred Heart of Jesus. If God returned me to her, she would form the League of the Sacred Heart of Jesus at our parish, St. Joseph's Church. I was there the day the league chapter was initiated.

We continued marching, another seven miles through clusters of forest separated by clearings, an area in Normandy that ran parallel to the coast. It was hot. Our gear was heavy. Morale was low. We were an invasion force, but no one knew where we were going, except the Officers in Charge, and they weren't telling. We were tired and hungry and there was a lot of grumbling.

"Fifteen minutes, men." First Lieutenant Charles gave the signal to stop and rest.

He got up on a small embankment in an area of sparse woods, took his carbine, one hand on the barrel, the other hand on the butt and raised it up over his head.

"Listen to me carefully," his voice boomed out and he had our attention. He was aware of the undercurrent of anger and rebellion among the men.

"I know before this war is over, some of my fellow officers will be shot in the back like dogs."

The men were startled. Some of them wondered how he could know that they were only waiting for the right moment to bring him down.

"Let the first coward step up and put a bullet in me. Don't shoot me in the back. I want to see the face of the yellow son of a bitch who wants to do me in."

No one moved. I had heard the rumblings. I had heard the malcontents the first night in the woods. One of the soldiers was a reputed sharp shooter. He also disliked authority, any authority. He led the plot to kill the first Lieutenant. One of the difficulties with replacement soldiers was they found it hard to form allegiance. Soldiers were dispatched from replacement camps, or repo depots, as needed, never as a unit. We were strangers with little or no time to make friends and another new Officer in Charge. There was no time to develop mutual respect between the ranks. We were soldiers without an outfit, about to replace a soldier who had become a casualty. We felt like cannon fodder.

The Lieutenant lowered his gun, took off the safety and cocked it. "I know who you are, if anyone is doing the killing, it will be me."

One of the men found a voice, "Lieutenant, I got news for you, no one's going to shoot you in the back."

For a moment we'd found a rallying point, a point of solidarity. We were still foreigners invading an occupied country, but we had something in common, we had a leader. A chorus rang out, "You're a good guy Lieutenant."

For the rest of the afternoon, the malcontents marched in front where we could keep an eye on them. We sang "When the caissons go rolling along" and then a round of "You're in the Army now" followed by "When Johnny comes marching home." I wasn't feeling half-bad and then we came upon the 90th Division. Lieutenant Charles signed me over to Captain Bremer. One of Bremer's officers delivered me to Sergeant Auwen, who grabbed my hand, gave it a few decisive shakes and said, "Howdy Private, you're the man I was missing, you complete my gun crew." Auwen was in charge of a 105 Howitzer.

Finally, I belonged to an outfit; I belonged to Sgt. James H. Auwen, a good old boy from Lexington, Oklahoma. He was over 6 tall feet, big square shoulders and blond hair. He introduced me to the rest of the guys in Charlie Company. We were seven in all. They were all dug in, the gun was dug in and that left only me. "Dig your hole, Varano." Sgt. Auwen commanded and handed me a shovel.

I dug a slit trench just long enough to lie in and just deep enough to hide in. It was quick work in the soft dirt. Dark clouds rolled in. I used my pack as a pillow, lay down just below ground level and began to doze. We waited for fire orders.

Although I would always long to be a pilot, I must express how much respect I had for the 105-Howitzer. This gun was an efficient piece of light artillery, a cannon, and I was a cannoneer. The gun had a range of 1-7 miles, and there were four 105's in our Battery. I was in "C" Company and there were also "A," "B" and "D" Company—Able, Baker, Charlie and Dog we were called. Willie was assigned to Dog Company. Together, we could fire a lot of shells, big, hefty shells, as fast as they could be jammed down the barrel. The infantry loved us. No wonder, they were the most vulnerable members of the Army and we protected them. This was all yet to come.

Back to my catnap, which was rudely interrupted by a thunderstorm. I was getting soaked as the shallow trench filled with water. Sgt. Auwen looked down at me, shook his head and threw a tarp at me. "Here Varano, cover yourself."

The rain stopped as quickly as it had begun. I was bailing out my trench with my helmet when I heard the drone of a German fighter plane. The pilot was flying so low, I could see his face in the cockpit, complete with leather helmet and goggles. He circled around our position, to get a good look.

Was ist das? What is this? He must have seen movement on the ground, and dived down to get a look. And now he saw American troops, just past the beach, already dug in. Without thinking, I jumped up and started firing my carbine, tracking just ahead of the plane, until I emptied my cartridge.

"Get down!" Sgt. Auwen yelled at me. Later, he chewed me another asshole.

"Varano, what the hell were you doing, you can't take down a plane with a pea shooter."

Our machine guns brought down the German plane. It burst into flames, shook the ground when it hit, one hell of a bang. The fuel ignited, an inferno dropped into our midst. The trees protected us from flying debris and ammunition that was going off like big firecrackers. Everyone wanted to see the downed German plane but we couldn't get any closer. Fire seared my face. Thick, black smoke and fumes stung my eyes, burned my throat, and there was a smell I would soon learn to recognize, the smell of burning flesh.

As soon as the flames subsided, a group of us ran toward the wreckage. A torso was all that remained of the German pilot. He had no head, arms or legs, just a charred slab of meat. The plane was a crumpled wreck of black metal. I could barely make out the Swastika on the tail.

This was my second day of combat, my first day with the 90th Division, 343rd Field Artillery Battalion (FABn), my first encounter with the enemy. I was close enough to see the man and then close enough to see him as debris. We were lucky that no other planes followed this German pilot. We figured he didn't know what he had seen from above, and when he dove down to find out, it was too late for him to escape our machine guns and ack-ack (anti-aircraft) fire.

This image stayed with us, the beginning of the carnage. "The end of our youth," Sgt. DeLeo, from Dog Company, called it. By now, fire orders had come down from the Command Post (CP). We ate K rations and tried to catch a few hours sleep between guard duty and before the shelling, which was scheduled to begin at 0500.

Chapter Three

Hedgerow Fighting

We were up at 0400 with a cup of coffee and K-rations and got into position for our first offensive against the Germans. We didn't sleep well, not just because we were lying in holes in the ground, open to the elements, but we were visited by a low flying German plane at 2300. CP instructed us to hold our fire, but we sure were itching to take this representative of the Luftwaffe out of the night sky. The drone began before we saw him, low and insulting. He was baiting us, daring us to reveal our position. We never once fired on Old Bed Check Charlie, who became a regular feature at 2300 during our nights of combat in France. You could set your watch.

It got light not much after 0500 because of our northern latitude in Europe, a few weeks from the longest day of the year. Ammo was already knocked out of the boxes and encased from the day before. I was on my gun in Charlie Company, and soon I could hear all four guns going off in our Battery, including Dog Company, Willie's gun. Orders went something like this: Charlie Company, 10 rounds, 4 miles, elevate 20 degrees, rotate 5 degrees right. It was not long before our seven-man crew was a smooth running machine.

The night before I had to calm Willie down after First Lieutenant Frank Lubinski had finished his little speech to our Battery. It was a combination put down, pep talk, prayer meeting that went something like this: "Just a reminder for you so-called cannoneers, I don't expect to see all of you after tomorrow's attack. Don't forget, you guys who are replacements, there's plenty more GI's waiting to replace you. Do your best out there, be careful, God bless." My first impression of Lubinski was a lasting one; he was a big, strong, pompous ass.

This first mission, we fired for hours, over a hundred rounds. Soon we'd used up the shells that had been prepared and stacked. Then it took two guys to knock the shells out of the boxes, two guys to insert the shells into the casings with one powder bag per mile, and one man to load the shell into the breach block. Sgt. Auwen relayed co-ordinates to the gunner Corporal that was George Verdel. George sited the gun, closed the block and yelled, "Fire" with a pull of the lanyard cord. The gun recoiled into the spikes, the siting was corrected to account for recoil, and the process started all over: encase, load, site, and fire. The most dangerous part of the process was loading. The shell detonator was in the nose. If the loader hit the block with the nose of the shell, instead of directing it into the breach, the shell could explode upon impact. Whenever someone hit the side of the block and we heard the clank, our hearts would leap in fear, but we never hit it hard enough because I'm still here.

Gunner Corporal was a demanding position, one that George Verdel earned, and I guess I earned his confidence. As far as I know, I was the only one who knew he had only one good eye. George was from Deer Park, Washington and we fought together throughout Europe. He was older than me and walked with a limp, but he qualified not only for the Army but also for the most technical position on the gun. George loved women and he loved to drink. When I returned from my five-day pass in Paris, I brought back the best booze I could find for George. He received the bottle of 5-Star-Cognac with reverence. He used to say to me, slightly apologetic, in a gravelly voice, "Don't get me wrong, John, but if I only had a good fuck right now and a nice bottle, I wouldn't mind dying in this muddy hole."

We were fighting in the hedgerows. How can I describe them? Balzac, the great French novelist of the 19th century, described the hedges in Normandy as banks of earth raised by the peasants to protect their fields and define ownership as the land was divided up. These mounds of dirt were formed in the shape of a flat ridge, as much as six feet tall and four feet wide. Beeches, oaks, and chestnut trees grew on top of the mounds. The roots intertwined in hedge walls, along with weeds, grass, and vines. The tree branches grew across the road, a road that was more like a moat, surrounded by tall, clay banks and old, snaky rooted, branching trees. These lines of hedges and sunken lanes crisscrossed each other and played tricks on the eyes. We were not prepared to fight in terrain like this, but the Germans were.

The Krauts were dug in and were not about to give up their defensive advantage. Our guys moved forward one hedgerow at a time, 50-100 yards to the next one, maybe two hedgerows a day. Infantry was not enthusiastic about getting shot or blown up by mortars, machine guns, or a land mine. Who wanted to leave their hedgerow to attack the Germans in the next one? They wanted those huge, Made-in-the-USA 105 MM shells dropping in front of them instead, right on top of the Germans.

Although we were right behind the infantry, we could not see through the hedges to our targets. We acquired targets from a Forward Observer (FO), who relayed coordinates to the Command Post (CP) by radio. The FO was sometimes an officer assigned to the position, sometimes an infantry man who got clearance to order his own fire mission. When infantry called in artillery they liked to order extra rounds, "for effect," once we'd hit the target. After all, the infantry dough boy was going to walk through the position we'd just hit. The FO had eyes on the scene. After he'd radio coordinates to CP, the Command Post relayed them to 1st Lt. Lubinski. Lubinski assigned the fire mission to Sgt. Auwen who gave directions to our gunner Corporal Verdel. That's how we knew where to direct our shells. The FO would radio back if we were short, long, to the left or right of target, and we would change gun sightings until we were on the money, and then 'boom,' a direct hit.

Sometimes all four 105-Howitzer companies in our Battery would fire on the same target, and working together like that, Able, Baker, Charlie and Dog could do some definite damage. When we finally took German prisoners, they complained vehemently about our 105's. They thought we shot them from machine guns, we pounded them so hard and fast.

The Germans answered with 88's and Nebelwerfers. It was like artillery duels. Nebelwerfers were not as accurate but it was a psychological weapon, non-parallel. The 88 was the finest German artillery piece of the war. It was fast, accurate, versatile, used as an ack-ack and an anti-tank gun. When the Germans opened fire, their mortars were bigger, louder, and their machine guns fired twice as fast. But the "screaming meemies" were the worst, the Nebelwerfer, the multiple rockets. It was a six-barreled gun that discharged high velocity shells. They screeched overhead and made you want to bury your head in the ground. So high pitched, so many at once, so fast, it made me and most everyone else just want to run and hide. A "screaming meemie" seemed to have my name on it, headed right for me, but I had to tough it out, stay with the gun. That scream gives me nightmares still.

After a week or two, we received orders to move the guns. The infantry had moved forward into the hedgerows, so we did too. But once in the hedges, we were blind as moles. Hedgerow combat was akin to fighting while lost in a maze. The infantry said they cleared out the Germans before we moved the guns up, but some enemy soldiers remained. One could never be sure what was on the other side of a hedge, a machine gun, a land mine, or a booby-trap.

We couldn't sleep; everything was so close. We could hear the German guns. We were jumpy with no release for our anger and fear. We forgot how to joke around. Like when Smittey said, "Hey Murph, you are getting to be a real lazy son-of-a-bitch," and without hesitation, Murphy picked up a piece of wood, the side of an ammo box, and buried it into Smittey's skull. Smittey lay there, unconscious, and the medics came to take him away. Murphy was transferred. No, there was no joking around, just shooting and being blown up and going nowhere except a few yards forward to the next hedgerow, or taken out of combat as a casualty or put in a body bag as one of the dead.

Harry wanted to know, "Why don't the goddamn Germans give up?"

We'd been firing day and night, round after round, the Howitzer tube sometimes got so hot we thought it would melt. We were a bit deaf, half-crazed, shell-happy.

"Encase, load, site, fire."

"They are the best-trained soldiers in the world," I answered.

"Whose side are you on Muzzy?" Muzzy was short for Mussolini. Harry Burgman from Clawson, Michigan didn't like me because I was Italian American. That is putting it mildly, he had murder in his eyes. After that, I kept quiet around Harry. The truth is, the Germans were better trained and better equipped.

Once, when there was a pause in the firing, an order came down from the CP, "Gas alert!" My gas mask was in my foxhole. I dove in and strapped it on. Half the guys could not find theirs. Either they had left them on the supply truck, or had discarded them when stripping off layers during the heat of the fire missions. During basic training I had to march through a tent filled with noxious gas. The split second before I got my mask on was enough exposure to give me the dry heaves and leave me coughing and choking. Some of the guys passed out and had to be pulled out of the tent during the drill.

That night in Normandy, many of us would have been dead, except it was a false alarm. The smoke from the shells, the dust from the exploding earth, the pollution from the gunpowder, the smell, it all mixed with the ground fog. The air was thick and stagnant with nightfall. It certainly got our adrenaline going and guys tried to keep their masks close by after that.

Another time, during a lull, Sgt. Auwen came up to me, "Varano, get your ass up here, I have an assignment for you."

While one of the Corporals drove the jeep, my job was to escort a fellow cannoneer to the field hospital behind the lines. He leaned on me during the entire ride, his eyes half-open and staring, he could not speak. We brought this GI, I think his name was Kelly, to the triage tent, supported his limp body between us, and then this Army doctor, a Major no less, tilted Kelly's face up by lifting his chin. With his thumb, the doctor pulled back an eyelid, Kelly's eyes were rolled back in his head. Then he slapped Kelly across the cheek with such violence that all I could do was react.

"Do that again and I'll kill you," I had my gun in the Major's stomach.

"Take it easy soldier, I just wanted to see if he was faking."

"You don't know what it is like on the front."

Kelly wasn't faking; they called it shell shock in World War I. Now they called it battle fatigue. Kelly did not respond to the abuse. He did not respond to anything. On my way back to the line, bouncing along in the jeep, I realized what I had done and was glad not to be facing a court-martial.

I should have felt lucky that I wasn't infantry. They were dying in the hedges. We were going deaf and going nuts, but we weren't getting direct fire, unless the German's located our guns. That is one reason we kept moving. I should have felt lucky, like the warrant officer said when he told me I'd flunked aviation. But every time I saw a formation of bombers, I wanted to be up there escorting them as a fighter pilot. I was resentful. The emotion never died from being denied my heart's desire to fight the war in an airplane. Here I was stuck in the hedgerows, and it felt like I was going to die in the hedgerows. The Normandy Invasion had proceeded as planned. Thousands of troops and tons of equipment were stacking up behind us, but we could not make substantial forward movement. Rommel nearly pushed us back into the English Channel. We threw everything at the Germans. Our planes bombed their supply lines, day after day. Gone was the advantage of surprise. The Krauts knew were, we were and they weren't budging, except one hedge to the left or one hedge to the right. The fields were mined to blow off the legs of the dough boys as they moved forward.

But then it seemed like a miracle happened. All those bombs we dropped on the supply lines, all those shells fired into the hedges, finally had an effect. Supply starved, shell-dazed Germans began to surrender. And they looked scared, disorientated, sweating in their leather. German soldiers were supposed to die before they gave up. But they knew that Americans were good to their prisoners, especially since the Germans had not raped our wives and burned our homes. Our families were safe across the ocean.

Fighting tactics were about to change.

Chapter Four

Campaign in Northern France

We broke through the Normandy hedgerows at St. Lo but only after we paid a high price. It began on July 24th, 1944. General Bradley commanded the operation. The day dawned in a thick overcast. The heavy bombers droned overhead, and they dropped their loads through the cloud cover. The bombs exploded tremendous, resonating booms, one after another. I turned to George Verdel and said, "Good thing they're on our side." But this day some of the bombs hit a bit off-target.

News passed quickly down through the 90th Division. American bombs had fallen on the 30th Division and wiped out an entire outfit. General Bradley blamed poor visibility and called off the bombing until the next day.

After we dug in our gun, Sgt. Auwen spoke up. "You know, you expect to get killed by the Krauts, but when you get killed by your own guys, there's something rotten in Denmark."

Auwen was a well liked and an efficient soldier. My favorite non-com (non-commissioned officer), Auwen was like a big brother to me. Auwen and I fought together through the war, in the five major battles in the ETO, along with George and Willie.

We grumbled a lot that night, and looking back on it now, I know that we were all seriously shaken to know that so many American soldiers had been killed or wounded by American bombers. I thought about my thwarted aspirations to be a fighter pilot, turned to George and said, "Fly guys get confused."

The next morning, July 25th, the weather cleared. Once again, General Bradley launched COBRA, the Army code name for this concentrated and massive aerial offensive. B-17s filled the skies, in formation, flying fortresses in groups of 12. Wave after wave, the bombers droned in and dropped clusters of bombs. 1000-pound bombs hit the ground on target. German artillery guns,

29

the 88's, knocked three of our huge B-17's out of the sky. American P-47s, our low-flying fighter plane, took out the 88's. They took out specific enemy targets, supply depots, and communications centers as identified by aerial spotters. Then it was my turn.

I helped to load, site, and fire shell after shell. Not just our 105-Howitzer gun company, but combined battalions of artillery fired as part of a concerted Corps attack. Three Divisions worked together, more than 45 guns, shooting simultaneous rounds as fast as we could load them for an hour straight. My ears still ring from that noise. We took out German gun positions, tanks, and trucks. Although badly shaken by casualties from friendly fire, American infantrymen pulled it together, as commanded. Before the smoke cleared, our foot soldiers moved forward. Soon, the Germans who had survived the bombing began to surrender. We had finally routed the German 7th Army.

Jeep drivers told us, acting as liaisons between headquarters and the front line, that American casualties continued to mount from the Allied bombing. Sgt. Auwen said, "What's the matter with those 90 day wonders, can't they pull their men out when they see they're getting killed by our own bombs?"

The next day, march orders came down from the CP. We moved forward and followed the infantry. We now moved forward in miles, not in yards, not the way we fought through the hedgerows. We fired on our appointed targets, the dough boys took new positions, artillery fired and cleared out the Germans. The infantry advanced.

On August 1st, Sgt. Auwen informed us, "We don't belong to Bradley anymore, now we're with Patton."

George growled, "What's the difference, Johnny, now we'll get killed today instead of tomorrow."

Between fire missions, I sought out my good buddy Willie, who said, "With Old Blood and Guts in charge, we'll be home for Christmas."

We were both optimistic when General George S. Patton took command of the 90th Division and we became part of his 3rd Army. I had followed Patton's exploits in Africa and Sicily. We watched newsreels through basic training in Fort Bragg that revealed Patton's brilliance. As a controversial figure, he was a favorite subject in the Army's daily newspaper, *Stars and Stripes*. When I was stationed in England, he was on a lecture tour, ostensibly in disfavor for slapping a soldier. Because of his big mouth, he was usually in trouble with the top brass, but that made me like him more. No one questioned his intelligence and bravery. He loved and understood war; he was a student of military maneuvers. He was an instinctive strategist. With him as our General, we were going to move. The Germans invented the blitzkrieg, but Patton redefined it. He didn't let me sleep. "Tired men win the war," he said. I was always tired.

With Patton's version of blitzkrieg, all hell broke loose. Tanks rumbled down the road with half a dozen infantrymen riding on the back. We fired our guns and the Germans retreated. When it was time to move to a new position, we hitched the Howitzer to the truck. Sgt. Auwen would jump in next to the driver. I think the driver's name was Jose, but we called him, "Hey Amigo." We traveled across France in the back of a GMC US Army two and a half ton 6X6 truck. It never broke down, not that I can recall, anyway, and we hauled the trusty Howitzer across the country, across the continent. Hey Amigo kept it running, he also delivered our ammo during fire missions. I knew I was lucky to be riding with the artillery instead of marching across France with the infantry. Sgt. Auwen broke through my reverie, "Varano, get your ass in the truck."

I climbed in the back and took my seat on the wooden plank next to George. We sat three on a bench and faced each other. Depending on the length of the ride, the six of us leaned against the metal frame for back support, or slumped forward to catch a few Z's. We traveled through French towns with names like St. Hilaire du Harcouet, Montaudin, Ernee and Moulay. That broke the monotony, especially if we spotted some French girls. Then George perked right up, "Wouldn't mind getting a piece of that ass."

Other times we'd just gripe. One of our favorite targets was 1st Lieutenant Frank Lubinski from Pennsylvania. All someone had to say was, 'Did you say Frank?' and we would launch into an abusive parody of the man. We called him jerk Lubinski or just 'that asshole.' We disliked him because he was conceited and domineering as he strutted around displaying his athletic physique. We disliked him because he made a big show of his authority. When it was time to move, Lubinski made a point of driving his jeep up and down the line, "Let's go." Then he would pump his fist up and down in the air and yell "Hubba, hubba," just to yank our chain. Behind Lubinski's back, the Italians answered, "el la faccia du" (in your face) with a reciprocal fisted salute, which included a bent arm pump and a simultaneous slap of the biceps.

We kept moving. Patton demanded it. We'd fire our guns, the next company would move forward to cover us, then we'd leap frog, all the while covering the infantry. Although, at the speed we traveled, we occasionally caught up with the dough boys.

Orders came down from the CP. An aerial spotter located a Tiger tank, the largest of the German tanks, a mile up the road. We had a target. We piled out of the truck, unhitched and positioned our gun, sited and fired three rounds. CP reported back, "You hit the tank." Everyone cheered.

"We got the Krauts." The Germans made the best tanks and we took one out.

"Okay guys, let's go, hubba, hubba," commanded Lubinski, with all his charm, answered by, "el la faccia du" after he moved down the line. We piled into the truck.

Up the road we met German infantry, cut off from their unit. They fired at us with machine guns. Our tank guns knocked them out, and the white flags came up. Sometimes, we moved so fast that scenes blurred together. We traveled as far as 70 miles in one day, like a bunch of site-seeing GI's, we crowded into the back of a Howitzer-towing truck, but the sites we saw were pretty bad—a bombed out countryside that resembled the surface of the moon. We rode in an open truck. It was hot and dusty. Sometimes we would get an order to fire, the order would be countermanded, and we'd have to pull up before firing a shot and keep on moving, bouncing down the road.

We traveled through French villages and saw the destruction. It seemed crazy. We were saving the French people from their German oppressors by blowing their country to bits, buildings leveled, trees uprooted, craters in the earth where bombs had exploded. Smoldering vehicles, tanks, and trucks clogged the roads along with dead and bloated farm animals and dead soldiers. The stench overwhelmed us. We moved so fast that we stayed ahead of mop-up operations. We suffered with the smell and the sight of the dead before the clean-up crew could tag and bag the bodies.

Townspeople were hung from lampposts if the Germans suspected them of being part of the Free French Forces. We saw the remains of a village population: women and children herded together in a barn, the barn doused with gasoline, and set fire. If they managed to run out of the burning building, their were bodies riddled with machine gun bullets. The Germans employed a Scorch Earth policy whenever possible, which meant as they retreated, they burned everything left behind.

The French people brought out food and drink to celebrate when we stopped in a village. Our presence meant the Germans were on the run. The cognac and wine flowed. The French women came out of hiding, throwing flowers, kissing our cheeks, crying and hugging us. George's response was "Ooh lala." If it wasn't for the obvious and vigilant presence of the MP's (Military Police), I am sure that George would have taken advantage of the gratitude of the French women. My heart went out to the old people and the children who had been hiding in caves and in holes they'd dug in the ground. They came out to see the Americans. We gave all the food we could to the hungry kids. "Chocolate, pour la mama et pour le pere. Hey yank." The kids knew how to beg.

"Hey Sarge," I said, "these kids are starving, look at them. They are skin and bones. We need more K-rations."

Auwen knew we were giving it away. He requisitioned more food from Staff Sgt. Michael Calo. Calo was a good Italian. He taught school back home in

Waterbury, Connecticut, my home state. He and I talked about news from home whenever we had a chance, especially after mail call. Calo was in charge of food supplies and he gave us whatever he could. We passed out a lot of candy.

When we stopped for the night, sometimes we slept in empty barns or deserted farmhouses. Sleeping in buildings saved us the time and energy it took to dig trenches, but it was dangerous. German soldiers would also hide in the buildings, separated from their outfit, wounded or just left behind. One evening, I was on guard duty outside of a barn. I heard noises, took the safety off my 30-caliber carbine rifle, and went to investigate. I crouched down and aimed through the partly open barn door. Lt. Lubinski pushed the barn door open and found himself in my gun site. "Don't shoot." he said, startled and taking a step back.

I recognized him, took my gun site off his chest, and pointed the gun up in the air. I followed Lubinski inside the barn while he tucked in his shirt and fastened his belt. Two naked women were sitting on green khaki Army blankets, chatting in French. One lit a cigarette, and they nonchalantly wrapped the woolen blankets around themselves when they saw me. "You didn't see anything, Varano."

"Yes sir!" I answered immediately.

Lubinski could and would put me in the infantry in the blink of an eye. With the 1st Lieutenant was a handsome and well-liked non-com Liaison Officer. His name was Jack.

I can't remember his full name. As he buttoned up his fly, he turned to me with his clear blue eyes, "I can count on you, Varano."

"You'd better believe it, Jack."

Lubinski and Jack were in the hay making hay and I had almost shot them because I had been trained to "shoot first, ask questions later" in this kind of circumstance. I had the feeling that Lubinski would just as soon have shot me after I took my gun site off him, but he and I both knew I could keep my mouth shut.

On the evening of August 12th, we had been ordered to dig in near the village of Damigni. I loved this part of Europe. As the sun set over the farmland, the peaceful light shone over the golden wheat fields and invited us to dig our holes for the night. First, we dug in the gun and cut down some wheat to cover it for camouflage. It was August, and the wheat stalks were tall. The field was ideal for digging; the ground was soft and loose, deep and loamy topsoil. We felt like we could dig down to hell, and that is what my trench partner, Edmund Jim from Tohatchi, New Mexico, almost did. We could stand up in the trench and still be underground. That is how deep Big Jim dug in that night. Jim was an American Indian, over six feet tall, strong and quiet. I wrote letters for him to mail back home. He spoke broken English. He was a good man and an excellent trench partner.

It was pitch dark, no moon, and time to rest. Big Jim had pulled the first shift of guard duty, and I had just settled into our trench when the drone of airplanes disturbed the night. At first I thought it was our guys, American planes, except that the sound was coming from the wrong direction. The planes dropped flares that ignited and lit up the sky. Then I knew it was not our guys; they would never give away our position. We were scared. The drone was deafening, and the formation of enemy planes was large and well organized.

Harry Burgam jumped into my trench. A member of my gun crew, Harry always harassed me. He blamed me for being of Italian descent, he blamed me for Mussolini's pact with Hitler, he blamed me for being young, for having all my teeth and addressed me as "Mussie, you dirty whop bastard!"

When he talked, it was a whine. Harry always had liquor hidden somewhere on his body. He was 30 or 35; it was hard to judge because his flushed face was so deeply creased. He had beady brown eyes, short-cropped dark red hair, and quite a few missing teeth. I usually refused to dignify his abuse with a response.

The night of August 12th, however, Harry was pleading with me, "Johnny, I don't want to die." He was crying and violently shaking. He grabbed me, squeezed me; the guy was falling apart, having a breakdown right in front of me. His tobacco stained teeth showed as his mouth screwed up in a grimace, the flares illuminated the tears streaming down his face. It was a horrible night, we had been traveling so fast we'd outrun the rest of the 90th and were isolated from our Division. Harry was hysterical. He begged, "Pray for me," and got down on his knees in my trench. I grabbed him and tried to calm him down.

Harry continued, "I know you are Catholic, I know you pray. I'm Catholic too, you know." So we recited Hail Marys through the bombing. We stayed alive that night by the grace of God and the extreme depth of our trench. We owed our lives to Big Jim and Captain Fred S. Bremer from River Forest, Illinois. He insisted on two things every time we stopped, "First, dig in the gun. Second, dig in yourselves."

As German bombs dropped around us, we not only heard them, we felt them. These were heavy bombs that could kill you from concussion alone. Finally, the shelling stopped as suddenly as it had begun, and we were still alive. Harry's attitude toward me changed after that. He no longer called me "Mussie, you dirty whop." I told no one about his breakdown.

I prayed my way across Europe. I cannot count how many times Willie and I prayed the rosary together. Mine was a black, wooden rosary with the figure of Christ nailed to the wooden crucifix. The cross itself was trimmed in gold-colored metal. When I faced death, I felt close to God, so I felt God's presence the whole time I fought in the Second World War. I prayed whenever

I could. Waiting in the trench, sitting in the truck, I'd reach into my left breast pocket where I kept the rosary, the one my mother gave me when I left for the service. I fingered those beads through some evil times. If I couldn't get to my breast pocket, I prayed in my head, kept count on my fingers, "Holy Mary, Mother of God, pray for us sinners, now and at the hour of our death, Amen," interspersed with "Glory Be's" and "Our Father's."

My mother taught me to pray the rosary as a youngster. I was drawn to the beads, the cycle of prayers, the repetition and the invocation of the Catholic faith with the Joyful, Sorrowful, and Glorious Mysteries. Growing up in St. Joseph's Parish in New Britain, Connecticut, I prayed the rosary during Friday night novenas. I attended regularly with my sister, Josephine and my mother, Grace. Praying the rosary gave me peace like nothing else could. One of the promises made by the Blessed Virgin to St. Dominic was, "Those who will recite my Rosary piously, considering its Mysteries, shall not die a violent death." I believed that.

Some of the older guys called me kid. I was only nineteen and it was my first time away from home, except for boot camp. But after a few weeks in combat, I was no longer a kid. Willie and I attended mass as often as we could. The chaplain who served the 343rd Battalion was a Belgium born Catholic priest, ordained in the US, but quite at home in Europe. He celebrated Mass wherever he could. It was sometimes in front of a barn with a jeep as the altar. I remember he wore white vestments, and we received General Absolution without even a chance to say, "Bless me Father for I have sinned . . . ." The priest blessed us and announced, "Your sins are forgiven you."

We received Holy Communion, "The Body of Christ," to which we answered, "Amen."

We needed to know that if we died the next minute, we died in a state of grace.

The day after the night bombing at Damigni, we received march orders and were back on the dirt road, bouncing along in the back of the truck. After several miles, I heard an explosion behind us. Suddenly, a loud cry came up the line, "Jump!"

Jose stopped the truck. Our ack-ack's started firing. Auwen yelled, "Jump for cover!"

There was another explosion up ahead to the left of the road. I was already in a ditch, having jumped off the truck on the first command. Within split seconds, a fighter plane dove down and strafed our column. I laid in the dirt, face down, flat on the ground, the ditch was only a few feet from the road, no more than a foot deep. Everyone was yelling. Machine gun bullets from the plane ricocheted all around, coming from behind, somehow missing me. The pilot came down so low, he could see that we were Americans. He pulled up and quickly disappeared.

"All Clear." The command came down the column and we jumped back into the truck and drove down the road. We passed the burning wreckage of the plane that had crashed to our left, about 250 yards from the road. Red-orange flames produced black, billowing smoke. Ammunition from the plane exploded like huge firecrackers. We wanted to see what happened, but we had to stay in formation. Soon enough, word came down the column. It was our own planes, P-38's, that had attacked us from behind. We were all emotionally wrought, after being attacked and almost killed by friendly fire. I tried to defend the Air Force, "after all, we all make mistakes." But I didn't feel so self-assured. My confidence in the fighter pilots was shaken. We couldn't stop talking about it.

The next day, Liaison Officers brought us the scoop, two P-38's had been circling above our column and thought we were Germans. One of the planes came down too low, and after shearing the tops of four telephone poles, it hit one of Baker Battery's gun section trucks with its wing and propeller, and the truck exploded. That was the explosion we heard just before the strafing started. Then the P-38 crashed and burned to the left of the road. Four men from Baker Battery were killed and two injured. The P-38 pilot was burned beyond recognition. That day we had fastened fluorescent orange plastic tarps to the hood of our trucks, tied down to the fenders. That was our identification system so the Allied airmen could identify us as Allied troops. The color changed regularly, and I guess we had the wrong colored panels on that day.

Finally, when we thought we couldn't take much more, we got some R and R. We had earned it. Our nerves were frayed. We were pulled off the line and replaced by fresh troops. We camped in a French field, did maintenance on the gun, and cleaned up. We got our water from a French farmer's well, and we'd put little brown tablets in it to make it drinkable. We washed clothes and washed ourselves. On the second day of rest and relaxation, we got acquainted with the farmer. He told us he sold wine to make a living.

Cpt. Bremer told Lt. Lubinski to buy a vat of wine for his men. The farmer arrived with a two-wheel oxen drawn cart and delivered a huge barrel of wine, enough for 100 men. It was mid-afternoon in August. The sun was hot, there was very little shade, and the guys started drinking. Everyone relaxed; some took their shirts off, laid their washed clothes out on the trucks to dry. Some soldiers slept, others played cards or wrote letters, and the wine continued to flow. Pretty soon the guys were singing, dancing, getting slaphappy. One guy had a harmonica, he played and we sang, "Over hill, over dale . . . we hit the dusty trail, as those caissons go rolling along." Guys started wrestling, impersonating Lubinski or their girls back home. The men horsed around and continued to drink. Pretty soon, many soldiers were falling down drunk. It didn't take a lot of alcohol, really, since everyone was tired and the sun was hot. Between 1800 and 1900, most of the guys appeared to be sleeping it off, pretty much dead to the world. Willie and I and a few other guys remained sober. We didn't drink for various reasons.

Suddenly I heard "swoosh" overhead and shells started to explode, not more than 100 yards away. Debris came raining down over our heads and we realized, "We're under attack!" German artillery shells were falling all around us. The phone rang from CP. I picked it up. "Fire Orders, enemy location, elevate 20 degrees, rotate 30 degrees left, fire 7 miles, 3 rounds."

I relayed the coordinates to George Young from Louisville, Kentucky since George Verdel, our gunner Corporal, was inebriated. Young ran out and set the citing pole, Big Jim knocked the shells out of the boxes and loaded the powder bags, I set the gun coordinates and we fired the Howitzer. CP called back to give us new coordinates to improve the accuracy of our hits. We loaded the gun, sited and fired at will for a good hour. Then the attack stopped. The men had sobered up. Under threat of death, sobriety returns quickly. We'd held our ground, stopped the enemy from making a breakthrough. Next day Liaison Officers brought the news. The 343rd FABN received accommodations. Here I thought we were going to be court-martialed or brought before the firing squad. But somehow a few sober men had managed to supply enough firepower to stop the German counter-attack. If I was sweating it, imagine how Cpt. Bremer and 1st Lt. Lubinski must have felt. They had been promoted on the battlefield, Bremer from 1st Lieutenant to Captain, and jerk Lubinski from 2nd Lieutenant to 1st. Bremer was trying to be a nice guy and reward his men for their bravery and allegiance by supplying alcohol during a rest period. We almost got blown away, not to mention that drinking was illegal for enlisted men in the Army. Inspectors came down from Division Headquarters (HQ) to investigate. HQ wanted to know how the Germans knew that 343rd was on R and R, five miles behind the front line? The French farmer was eventually identified as a German spy. Not one word was spoken of our drunkenness.

Captain Bremer was a different commander after that. No more Mr. Nice Guy. If he caught anyone drinking, that soldier was put on ditch digging duty or latrine digging details. John Weinhardt from Los Angeles, California was almost always in trouble after that. He was an experienced combat soldier and we needed him, but he sure spent a lot of time digging ditches. He was a drinker. He'd get in a fight over some local French girl, he'd be digging latrines, then go AWOL, then get hauled back to ditch digging duty. He usually had a black eye or two.

Early in the French campaign, my field artillery battalion was chosen to be part of Special Task Force Weaver. The Task Force was a select group that probed the enemy line to find weak spots. We'd fire a few shells. If we'd get counter-attack, we would know that it wasn't a soft spot, chart the enemy presence, and move to the next position. We'd fire a few more shells. If there was no response, we'd move forward into enemy territory. On this particular mission, we probed and shelled with no enemy response. We continued to move forward in an effort to make contact. Suddenly, shells were exploding behind us.

Sgt. Auwen started yelling, "Hey, guys, we've been sucked in. It's a trap! Damn! What the hell is going on? Turn the gun around! This goddamn Army doesn't know its ass from a hole in the ground. Major Harris did it again! That son of a bitch is going get us all killed!"

We had to do a 180-degree turn of the Howitzer. We did it in seconds, but shells were now exploding from every direction. We were surrounded. Trees on all sides blocked our view. We received fire data coordinates from HQ in a matter of minutes. We were still connected by radio. We fired the gun as commanded. Sgt. Auwen had the radio pressed to his ear and was yelling out co-ordinates between expletives. But it was no use, we were woefully outgunned. Sgt. Auwen sent the message to Division HQ. "Weaver's task force is trapped. Send air assistance."

The US Army 8th Air Force came to our rescue. P-47's blasted open a corridor for us to get back in position. Boy, were we sweating it, the P-47's came flying in low, they could pinpoint the German artillery by the gun flashes. As they swooped down, they strafed the enemy positions and dropped their bombs on designated targets. We couldn't see the bombs, but we felt them, heard them, and smelled them. The air filled with smoke, and our feet felt the earth move as shock waves went through our bodies. The infantry sustained many casualties, but the majority of Task Force Weaver escaped from enemy territory. Major Harris was famous for his sense of misdirection. At that moment, without reservation, we all loved the 8th Air Force.

General Patton's blitzkrieg push-forward-at-all-cost strategy necessitated the coordination of ground troops, artillery fire, and air cover from Allied bombers. The plan was brilliant and effective. Then, suddenly, we were not getting our fuel rations. Patton's troops had outrun the supply lines. We were running out of gas.

Chapter Five

Double Crossing the Moselle

First Lieutenant Frank Lubinski gave the order, "Position the guns in front of these houses."

We were in France, outside of Metz, a city so heavily fortified by the Germans that it was known as Fortress Metz and protected by twenty-eight forts. The forts were constructed by the Germans to include moats, barbed wire, underground passageways, and gun emplacements made of reinforced, poured cement, the infamous pillboxes. Although Fortress Metz could not be overpowered, General Patton's 3rd Army, to which I belonged, had the city surrounded. Cold, November rains soaked our drab uniform fatigues to the skin. Nearly seven inches of rain fell during November in the Metz area of France, 1944. We ate, slept, and worked in the mud. The Moselle swelled in its banks, and it was still raining as the 90th Division prepared to cross the river.

Sgt. James Auwen turned to me, "Hey, Johnny, Lubinski is trying to win points, putting us up in a house. Now all we need is some French mademoiselles and a bottle of cognac. Maybe he's not such a dumb Polack after all."

I helped the other five guys in my gun company drag and push our 105-MM Howitzer through the mud and into position. There were four Howitzers in Charlie Battery. We kept them 50 yards apart so that the Germans couldn't blow up all the guns with one shell. I tossed a camouflage net over the Howitzer so that it blended into the scenery and hurried out of the rain into the abandoned building. It was a two-story house, partly furnished. I had just set my pack down in a corner of the living room, fantasizing about a good night's sleep, when Auwen ordered us outside for last minute checks on the gun. It was getting dark fast.

Captain Fred S. Bremer walked by, charts in hand, flanked by his aides, to inspect the gun emplacements. Bremer looked at the gun, looked at the house, and looked at Lubinski. Then, between clenched teeth, he tore into his 1st Lieutenant. "What the fuck's the matter with you? Can't you follow orders? The Germans will pick us off like sitting ducks. Are you deaf, dumb and blind? You are going to get us all killed."

Bremer extended his arm with a snap and pointed, "Put the guns over there," and turned on his heel.

We started to complain bitterly and loudly as soon as Bremer was out of earshot, but I'd never seen him that mad. Verdel was the bandleader. "That son of a bitch, Bremer, I'll bet you he has a warm, goddamn place to sleep tonight. What's he bucking for now, to make Major? The one night we're going to be nice and dry and that cocksucker kicks us out in the mud and rain. Look at that sweet mother-fucking corner I have for myself."

While we pissed and moaned, we moved as fast as we could, pulled the gun out of the mud, ripped off the camouflage net. Jose Alcorta, affectionately known as Hey Amigo, our trusty Texan truck driver and auto mechanic, backed up the truck, while we closed up the spades. As soon as the gun was hitched, I grabbed my gear from out of the house, jumped into the back of the truck, and Hey Amigo drove us 180 yards up river. Auwen was barking out the whole time, "Move your ass, get the lead out."

Minutes later, a tremendous blast burst overhead. Enemy artillery shells from German 88's filled the air, exploding nearby. The ground shook. I turned around. The houses were rubble.

"Who wants to be warm and dry now, you stupid assholes?" Auwen questioned. Then he was on the radio and got our fire data orders. We unhooked the gun, set the sights and were shooting back at the Germans. Shells sailed back and forth across the river, for close to three hours. By the time it was over, the Howitzer gun barrel was so hot I could boil water on it and Captain Bremer was our hero once again. The consensus in Charlie Battery was that he should be promoted, on the spot, to Brigadier General.

Willie Tushar, my best buddy, found me the next morning. "Hey Johnny, that prick Lubinski nearly killed us all."

Willie was also in Charlie Battery, but with a different gun crew. We'd been together since training camp in Barry, Wales.

"Yeah, Willie," I answered, "the son of a bitch is going to catch a bullet between the eyes one of these days. The only reason he's still alive is that when he hears incoming, the yellow belly is the first one to hide."

Willie nodded in agreement. "Bremer tore him a new asshole yesterday, didn't he? At least we won't see Lubinski for a couple of days, while he licks his wounds." We both laughed.

I had enlisted in this war to fight the Germans. My father had fought in World War I, and I'd grown up on his war stories. I considered becoming a career man, but first things first; the enemy was waiting for us on the other side of the Moselle. The Krauts had blown up one pontoon bridge after another, built by the engineers of the 90th Division. First we'd been stalled in Metz, when we'd run out of gas, along with the rest of General George S. Patton's Third Army. Now the weather had us by the balls, and all plans to be home for Christmas were gone.

Willie and I had been so hopeful when Patton first took over the 90th Division and we raced across France. As direct support to infantry, my position on the gun crew of the 105 Howitzer, a light artillery cannon, kept me several miles behind the front line. But as part of Patton's blitzkrieg across France, sometimes we'd find ourselves bouncing along in the back of the truck, a few minutes behind the infantry.

Willie and I parted, and since we were still waiting for the next fire mission, I decided to grab forty winks and huddled down in my trench. A light rain was falling. My thoughts returned to the summer in France, maybe in an unconscious effort to get warm. It was a quiet, moon lit August night. The 343rd Field Artillery Battalion had completed a fire mission and had received march orders. It was 0200; time to move out. Patton never would let us rest. Charlie Battery's trucks had slowed down as we'd moved through a town, the rubble still smoking from exploded shells. I thought, so this is what I just blew up. I wondered how many dead civilians were buried under the ruins.

Then we saw the bodies, caught in rigor mortis. The fighting must have ended with hand to hand combat in the streets because the men had fixed bayonets on their rifles. Silvery moonlight illuminated the dead soldiers; their unseeing eyes still open. We were ahead of the cemetery crew. I saw a dead German soldier, standing up, leaning against a building where he'd been shot. The corpse was supported by a low wall beside him and a pile of rubble up to his knees. His Mauser was still under his right arm, the muzzle resting on the ground like a crutch. I saw an American GI, sitting with his M-1 on his lap, leaning back against a half wall that just supported his head. There was a bloody wound on the left side of his chest, and a stain spread across his uniform until the blood coagulated. His blank stare looked out, most likely in the direction of the man who'd killed him. We saw dead soldiers draped over walls, in both American and German uniforms. As we crept through the town, we passed corpses scattered along the main street. Everything was quiet that balmy August night, and the gruesome battle remains were bathed in moonlight. No one on my gun crew spoke for a long while. We were spooked.

That scene still haunts me: the summer night, the moonlight, the ghastly corpses strewn about the silent town. The only movement was the smoke, rising from the rubble.

My reverie was interrupted by a command from my Sergeant. "Hey, Varano, heads up, fire mission." and with those words, Sgt. Auwen brought me back to the job at hand. I shook myself and crawled out of the slit trench where I'd been half-dozing in the cold November drizzle, no longer disappointed about leaving the house that had been blown up, but still miserable out in the weather.

We huddled around Auwen, like football players gathered around the coach. "Okay, here's the dope, fellas. At 1900 hours, we shoot ten rounds at the German guns across the river. And we keep firing until we get the order to stop. Tonight, the dough boys are going across in row boats, real quiet like, while we keep the Krauts occupied," Auwen went on, with his Oklahoma drawl.

"Aren't you guys glad you're not infantry? A row boat on this river?"

Shoot, we were all glad to not be infantry, and me, I couldn't even swim, almost drowned in the English Channel on D-day, even before I crawled up on Omaha Beach. Lubinski threatened to put me in the infantry, every chance he got, and he had the authority to do it. He was the number two man in "C" Battery. From what I could see, dough boys didn't last very long.

That night, however, most of the infantry got across. We heard the scuttlebutt the next day. Only a few boatloads got washed away in the current. The next night we shot another ten rounds at the German gun emplacements, and then kept on, "firing for effect," as the infantry called it. Division engineers worked doggedly in the dark to build a pontoon bridge across the river. Now that infantry had a foothold on the other side, the plan looked like it might work. The following night, after another 10 rounds of artillery shells were fired, we were ordered to pack it up. We hitched up the gun and loaded ourselves into the truck. Sgt. Auwen told Hey Amigo, "Once they let us on the bridge, drive as fast as you can."

If only they would let us on the bridge. We waited two hours in a long line while tanks, supply trucks, and transportation vehicles rumbled by. George Verdel, senior member of the gun crew, spoke for us all when he grumbled, "This goddamn Army, all we ever do is hurry up and wait."

Lubinski drove up and down the line of trucks, in his jeep, with his usual words of wisdom and consolation, "You men better pray you get across before you get hit."

George turned to me, "That suck-ass Frank, let me see him pray, when I get him on his knees and put a bullet between his eyes." We all laughed. Lubinski was always good for a joke as he strutted his stuff up and down the convoy. Someone chimed in, "Did you say Frank?" and our little group broke into parodies of the man.

As if he'd heard us, Lubinski headed back to our company.

"Let me see your carbine, Varano."

I handed him my 30-caliber rifle. He removed the magazine, sighted it, inspected the barrel, and handed it back to me.

"This gun is dirty. Are you trying to kill your whole crew? Clean it, now."

"Yes, sir." I went through the motions of cleaning an already clean gun.

"What a royal asshole," Verdel muttered, shaking his head.

Finally, we were directed onto the pontoon bridge by the MP's. Auwen rode shotgun, up in the cab with Hey Amigo, while the rest of us huddled in the back. The truck bobbed up and down as Hey Amigo drove as fast as traffic would allow. The wild river rushed by on either side of the floating bridge. It was raining and the canvas was rolled down over the back of the truck. I prayed to the Holy Family, Jesus, Mary and Joseph. I prayed to the Holy Trinity, the Father, the Son and the Holy Ghost, and I knew Willie was praying in the truck behind me. It took no more than fifteen minutes to get over, but the waiting resumed once we got to the other side. We were ordered to allow a tank battalion and supply trucks to pass. As soon as we were off the road, if you could call the muddy path through river bottomland a road, we were stuck in the mud. It had been raining for weeks. Our truck was a 2½ ton 6x6. Hey Amigo had put on tire chains for traction, but we could not move. It was 0100, welcome to Germany. Shells exploded nearby, sending up fountains of mud, and a tank had to be called up to winch us out.

Lubinski observed us getting pulled out of the muck and advised, "Heads up everyone, there's Krauts all around us, we're in Heine territory now."

Our first night in Germany, but there was no celebration, even though we were finally out of Metz and across the Moselle River. We were still wet, cold, and miserable. We were in the Fuhrer's Homeland. The tension was tangible, more solid than the darkness, than the mist that hovered over the river valley, or the mud that slipped under our wet boots. The way that I coped with misery and fear was to ignore it. We all kind of shut down after so many months under enemy fire, life without comfort and with a lot of hardship.

It was 0300 by the time we positioned and dug in the gun and dug our trenches. Once again, I pulled first guard duty, and the light drizzle turned to rain. Big Jim, the Indian from New Mexico, was my partner. We crouched in the trench with a 50-caliber machine gun, sitting back to back. That way we had a 360-degree view as we scanned the terrain, trying to familiarize ourselves with sounds and smells as our night vision kicked in. We kept each other company, quiet, tense, and alert.

Uneventful guard duty is exhausting, and when I was relieved, I dropped into the slit trench that I'd dug into the black, fertile river basin soil, at the base of a little hill. In a minute, I was asleep, wrapped in my GI coat with a GI blanket as a mattress, one edge folded over for a pillow. It was my first night in Germany, the first of many, but I wasn't thinking of the future, I only wanted a few hours sleep. Sleep deprivation breeds a certain type of soldier: docile and mechanical.

Next thing I remember, George Verdel was shaking me, "Come on, Varano, get up! You going to sleep your life away? You're going to drown down there like a rat."

I came to, the light rain had turned into a downpour, and I'd slept through it. There were six inches of water in my trench, the other guns in our Battery had started firing against the Germans, and I slept through it. Good thing George woke me up. Guys had been known to die in their sleep, drowned in their own slit trench. I crawled out of the wet hole and moved to my gun position. It was less than ten feet away. Mud covered my uniform; my clothes stuck to me. Water sloshed inside my boots, but at least the rain had washed the mud off my hands and face. Rain hit my helmet like the drumming sound of a tin roof. I was in position for my first fire mission on German soil, or more accurately, in German mud.

It began at 0700. The Howitzer recoiled in the mud, until the two spikes that usually held the gun firmly during a fire mission were completely submerged. The gun was unstable, inaccurate, because of the recoil after each shell was fired. The cannon sank so deep in mud, we had to call Jose to hook us up to the winch on the front of the truck and crank the gun out. Big Jim and George Verdel hauled in some big chunks of wood, and we wedged them against the spikes before our next fire mission.

A few days after we crossed into Germany, we got mail call. I received a packet of letters, tied with coarse brown twine. Most of them were from my sister Josephine. She wrote every night. I opened a pale green, lightweight airmail envelope and read:

Dear Johnny, September 9, 1944

Happy birthday, big brother. Everyone sends their love, including your big sister Florence, little brother Vinny, and of course Mama and Papa. Mama baked your favorite, chocolate cake with vanilla pudding between the layers and chocolate icing. We ate it all because it wouldn't have made it through the mail. How does it feel to be 20 years old? Just think, you aren't legal drinking age but you are killing the Nazis in Europe . . . Mama had a dream. In it she says "You're no more where you were before. You're now in a new country." I hope this is a good omen . . . I miss you, and Mama and I pray for you every day. Be safe. Come home soon so you can get your birthday presents.

All my love,
Josephine

As soon as I saw Willie, I told him, "I got a letter from home. Mama had a dream that we're in Germany."

Willie grimaced and shuddered. "Geeze, Johnny, one day your mama is going to write and say that I've been killed."

I grabbed his shoulder and patted him on the side of the face, "Hey buddy, don't worry, we'll be killed together," and we both laughed.

The weather let up, and Willie and I were given permission to go into town. We walked along the road, which was clogged with military vehicles. Someone had hit a land mine. Traffic was backed up from the booby trap and the road was pockmarked with small craters from exploded shells. It took us maybe half an hour to get to town.

We walked through the streets, taking in the sights, and saw a house that was still standing, although the windows were blown out. Looking through the shell holes, I could see that the walls were made of thick, gray cement. The Germans built good homes.

The front door stood open and Willie and I walked inside, out of curiosity, and moved from room to room. We came upon a young woman in a rocker. She started out of her chair when she saw us. We looked pretty scruffy, a lot like Willie and Joe in Bill Mauldin's comic strip, "Up Front." She had blood on her chest and was holding a baby. There was fear in her eyes. The Germans had been indoctrinated that Americans were savage animals.

The woman didn't move, except to hold out her baby to us, and then clutch it back to her breast. I could see the baby was dead. We used sign language to tell her we'd go get help. I didn't speak German then, but she seemed to understand. "Uno momento," I said in Italian and gestured with my hands. She smiled as tears streamed down her face.

"Let's get out of here," Willie said.

"That baby is dead. We have to get help for the mother," I said.

We went and found a medic. "There's a woman in that house. She needs help."

We waited outside for the medic to finish. "Hey Doc, what's the story?" We called all the medics "Doc" because they saved lives.

The medic spoke German and he told us that the woman had hid in the closet after the town had been taken because she was afraid, and yes the baby was dead. Shrapnel had hit them both.

To this day, I wake up in the night with a picture of that German woman, terror in her eyes, tears running down her face, holding out her dead baby, "Sehen meine Baby?" She clutches it back to her bloody chest, and accuses me with her eyes, "See what you've done?"

I prayed for forgiveness. Bless me Father, for I have sinned, I have killed innocent babies at their mother's breast.

The next day, the chaplain arrived at our battalion. He was a Catholic priest from Belgium, and after we celebrated a short outdoor Mass, I asked the chaplain if I could speak to him, a personal matter. He took me aside, and bowed his head while I explained how Willie and I had found the civilian woman and her dead infant.

"Father, we had just shelled that town, it was probably my Howitzer that killed that baby when a round exploded and sent shrapnel into that woman's chest. I cannot live with myself as a murderer of infants at their mother's breast."

The priest looked up at me, and he chose his words carefully. "Private Varano, the innocent as well as the guilty are punished in war. You did not put a gun to that woman's chest and pull the trigger. You are not a murderer. Say your act of contrition and know that God forgives you in this terrible time of war."

I was relieved after talking to the chaplain. I was drawn to him, as I was drawn to the priesthood. My experience in Europe only increased my desire to serve God. Each little town in France had at its center a church or a shrine, maybe a large crucifix. I prayed constantly. I found strength in my faith that I was an instrument of God, I surrendered my will to Him, and I wish I had been called to join the priesthood. Nothing would have made me happier. But I knew my own limitations, and I was just a regular Joe in the service in spite of the fact that some of the guys sought me out for comfort on religious matters. It must have been because I kept my cool, didn't swear and carouse, and seemed to have a center of conviction. I owe that to my loving family, my Catholic upbringing, and good experiences with the Church. That is how I got the occasional nickname of Father John.

All introspection evaporated when the medics arrived that afternoon to give us our shots. We were in mud up to our knees, living and fighting in the mud, when Sgt. Auwen belted out, "Line up, drop your pants, and show your ass. Everyone gets a shot."

If I had any modesty among men before basic training, the Army had systematically eliminated it. I loosened my belt, dropped my uniform fatigue trousers and bared my ass. I was oblivious to this form of degradation.

Harry Burgam, the whiner, was cursing up a storm. "Aren't you going to say something, Varano?" I just shrugged my shoulders and thought, what's the point?

I had an hour before guard duty. I wrote a letter home to Josephine. Although we all spoke Italian at home, I did not read or write it. Jo translated my letters to Mama and Papa.

Dear Josephine, October 15, 1944

Thank you for the birthday letter, Jo, you make me laugh, and Mama, you are right, we are in Germany. I don't know if the censors will let you read this. I am blessed to have a loving family back home and I feel your prayers. We had mass today, so I feel certain that I am in a state of grace. The chaplain read Luke 11:9-10, one of my favorite passages. "And so I say unto thee: Ask and it shall be given; seek and ye shall find; knock and the door shall be opened. For everyone who asks shall receive; he who seeks shall find; and to him who knocks, the door shall be opened unto him." We got our shots today, right on schedule, so don't worry Mama, I will not get a communicable disease. Willie and I had passes to go to town because there was a break in fire missions . . . don't worry about me, I am safe.

Love and prayers,
Johnny

I addressed the envelope and got ready for guard duty. Sergeant Auwen interrupted me with new orders. "Varano, you lucky son of a bitch, you got an hour to clean up, get in dress uniform, and get your ass in gear. You're going to Paris."

It turns out, my number had been drawn out of 1500 men in my battalion. One minute I am preparing for guard duty in a slit trench in Dillingen, Germany, and the next I'm packing with a five-day pass to Paris, the lovers' capitol of the world.

Verdel turned to me, "Don't it beat all, Father John goes to Paris, you lucky son of a bitch. The least you can do is bring me back a four star bottle and if possible, bring me a nice French Mademoiselle from gay Pare-EE."

Harry, the drunkard, was near tears with indignation. "It should be the old guys that go, not the young ones. But maybe you'll get lucky, get fucked, come back a man."

I washed, shaved, dressed, and within the hour was at Battalion Headquarters where I joined an assembled group of GI's. We climbed into a troop transport truck. I was battle weary. All six of us lucky GI's fell asleep during the long, bumpy ride. Back over the Moselle River, uneventful this time, since the territory was in Allied hands, but the trip took over five hours. We had to stop at all the checkpoints, but our driver knew the passwords and all our papers were in order.

We arrived in Paris just as dawn lit up the old city, a cultural center for art and romance, and a political center rich in religious and municipal history. Our truck stopped in front of a high-class hotel. I think it was called Le Royal. The Transportation Officer handed me furlough papers and script money. The six of us walked up to the desk and got our room keys. The carpet was a deep maroon and so thick it was like walking on a cushion—I could hardly believe it after the dirt and mud I had been living in for months.

A bellboy carried up my duffel bag and the maid unlocked my door. She left my key on the nightstand and indicated a buzzer that I should use to summon her. I washed and went down for breakfast in the hotel café. What a meal it was: French toast with honey, hash brown potatoes, coffee, juice, two eggs sunny side up. This hotel's bread and butter were American soldiers on leave, and they made a special effort to give us an All-American breakfast. I hadn't eaten like this in so long, it was too much, and although I wanted to wolf it down, I had to eat it slowly. My eyes were bigger than my stomach. I was used to cold K-rations and had a hard time with such a luxury.

I returned to my room, took a long, hot shower and as hard as I tried, I could not keep from falling asleep on the big comfortable bed; white satin sheets; feather pillows—what a change from the cold, hard, damp ground. I struggled awake by mid-afternoon and saw that my uniform had been washed and pressed, laid out on the chair for me, a woman's touch. I thought I should remember to tip the maid. I dressed and went out to eat in a sidewalk café where I ordered soup, steak and potatoes, bread and coffee and topped it off with exquisite French pastry. I felt like royalty. I strolled around Paris until dark, soaking up the ambiance. Then I went to a French Burlesque Show in an area that GI's nicknamed "Pig Alley." Pigalle, the red light district, was where I found La Folie Bergere, a club that catered to Americans. I looked out over the audience, a sea of faces, all U.S. servicemen. I sang along with "Mon Cherie," Marlene Dietrich's "Underneath the Lamppost" and a rousing rendition of "When Johnny Comes Marching Home."

The next morning I was up early and ate breakfast at the same outdoor café. Then I flagged down a taxi and told the driver, "Take me to Notre Dame Cathedral."

I went up to pray at the main altar and then climbed the 387 steps to the top of the tower—what a panoramic view of the city. I thought of Charles Lawton and "The Hunchback of Notre Dame." In my opinion, Notre Dame Cathedral is the most beautiful church in France. I felt the presence of God and was awed by the sense of centuries of worship within the historic gothic walls. They spoke to me with reverence and royalty, power and wealth.

In the cathedral tower, while I was taking in the sights of Paris, I met an Air Force officer, also on leave, and we hooked up. He introduced himself as Bernard Winters from Toledo, Ohio, and I could not have found a better traveling companion. He seemed to know everything about the city and its history, a veritable walking encyclopedia. We went to The Louvre, and the painting that impressed me the most was the Mona Lisa. Her beauty haunted me, her hands were so real, and her gaze did seem to follow me around the room.

That night I went to an indoor café recommended by fellow GI's as the place to have a good time in Paris. I sat alone, nursing a beer for appearances, although I barely sipped it. At the time, I didn't like beer. A GI walked unsteadily towards me, "Mind if I sit down?" he asked.

"Go ahead," I answered, gladly. I did not want to be alone. He was at least ten years older than me, appeared to be in his early thirties and was quite disheveled. His dress uniform identified him as a member of the engineer corps, but his tie was pulled to the side, the top button of his shirt was gone, his cap was on sideways and his shirt pocket was ripped. He introduced himself as Richard, "But you can call me Rick," and stuck out his hand for a sloppy but enthusiastic handshake.

"My name is John. Glad to meet you," I said, and I really was. I needed someone to talk to that night, someone with whom to share the excitement of Paris. As American soldiers in Europe, Rick and I felt an immediate camaraderie.

"Hey buddy, can you spare a cigarette?" Rick had noticed that I carried a pack in the top left pocket of my Eisenhower jacket. I lit one for Rick and one for myself, although I just held it without taking a drag. He told me that a hooker had rolled him and that he was broke. He certainly looked beat up, so I ordered him a beer, although it was hard to tell if anything he said was true.

"Do you think we could get those girls to join us?" Rick motioned towards a pair of young beauties sitting at a table near the bar. I had my doubts, but Rick winked at them and they got right up and walked to our table. Rick's beer arrived, he motioned to the girls, and they seated themselves on our laps.

They were gorgeous. But I was uncomfortable with the black-haired young lady who had chosen to sit on my lap, so I offered her the chair next to me so I could study her. A woman this beautiful would not give me the time of day back home. But that night in Paris, I was in uniform, an experienced soldier, a liberator, pulled off the front line for some R&R. I had a wallet full of money. I was still a tired GI, but by this time I was in a pleasant state of shock. Using my French phrase book, I learned her name was Maria and introduced myself. She was exquisite. She had ivory skin and small hands, delicate features. Her quick smile revealed even white teeth and high cheekbones. She threw her head back and her hair tossed like the dark mane of an untamed filly. Her eyes were dark brown and her lips were full. I did my best not to stare but I was captivated.

Rick learned that the blonde girl on his lap was Monique. I ordered a round of drinks for our table, and Rick bummed another cigarette so I gave him the pack. With halting French and sign language, Maria and I communicated. I managed to ask her where she was from and she answered, "Italia." We dropped the awkward French and started speaking Italian. I told her my parents were born in Italy and that I'd lived there for a year when I was seven years old. Maria's family had migrated to France with thousands of other Italian laborers. She was only 17. I told her I had just turned 20. We talked and laughed, shared stories about our childhood, our parents, sisters and brothers, and life in the United States and Italy.

At the same time, Monique was warming up to Rick. We moved on to a restaurant and I bought dinner. Rick toasted me as their gracious host. I relaxed and even drank a glass of wine with dinner.

"Do you think we and the girls could get rooms somewhere?" Rick asked. "Sure," I answered. I did not want to break up the party. I could not remember when I had felt this good. From the looks of Rick, he needed me to take care of him. He had described his misadventures in Paris. The first night of his furlough he'd gotten drunk, rolled, and was awakened the next morning at the western end of the Champs-Elysees. He was near the Tomb of the Unknown Soldier when a French constable, a forgiving gendarme, sent him on his way. I realized that Rick mooched off GI's like me who needed company. He was a happy drunk and had managed to stay out of jail.

We walked the streets of Paris. It was an autumn night but it felt like summer. All the hotels were full, some with a line of GI's waiting for a room. We didn't go back to Le Royal that night because girls were not allowed up in the rooms.

I was ready to give up and call it a night when Monique said that she had a friend in one of the hotels. We slipped past the line; I greased quite a few palms. I was the moneyman; loaded with script money, GI issue, and it had a high exchange rate. I asked for two rooms, got the keys, and gave one to Rick. The maid showed us up to the second floor. Monique knew her way around and Rick clung to her as they disappeared into their room and shut the door.

I stopped. It was the first time I was alone with Maria. She took my hand and led me into the room and closed the door. The suite was decorated with burgundy and gold wallpaper, plush gold carpet, and fresh flowers on the bureau next to a large poster bed. In my naiveté, I'd assumed that one room was for the guys and one for the girls. I was scared, masquerading as a big shot GI, throwing money around, buying drinks and dinner, passing out smokes, booking hotel rooms. Maria and I had been talking for hours in Italian as if we'd known each other for years, but I could not be alone with her in this room. I'd never been with a woman. For Christ's sake, I had wanted to be a priest but felt that I wasn't smart enough, that God hadn't called me. After surveying the room, I turned to confess all to Maria, to tell her this was all a mistake. She stood before me naked. Before I could speak she walked into my arms and wrapped herself around me. Her breasts were soft and firm; the nipples stood out dark brown against the ivory of her skin. Her thick hair fell in waves over bare shoulders. The bedside lamp offered soft illumination that caught in her dark hair like a halo. She was an angel. Her pubic hair was even darker, and her eyes glowed. A light sheen of sweat glistened from her forehead and stomach. I'd never seen a naked woman. My body responded. She embraced me and I was ashamed. "Maria, I, I . . ."

She took my hand and guided me to the bed, pulled down the covers and laid me down. "It's okay, Giovanni, I will take care of you, sleep if you are tired." She unlaced my boots and removed them, along with my socks. She unfastened my belt, unbuttoned my pants and shirt, and took them off. I lay quietly, without protest, while she undressed me, slowly, and spoke softly to me in Italian. My heart was pounding. She kissed my fingers and stroked my arms; she kissed my eyelids, brushed my lips with hers, and kissed my forehead. I began to relax. Her fingers traced around my eyes. She removed my undershirt and my boxer shorts. The coolness of her fingertips traced the line of my jaw, her other hand moved lightly down my chest, resting on my stomach. My excitement grew. I had never been this aroused before. I took in a deep breath, and exhaled slowly.

"Don't worry sweet Giovanni." Maria spoke softly and sweetly in Italian. "Non si domenticare Giovanni."

She massaged the knotted muscles of my neck and shoulders. Her healing hands moved over me. Then her hands moved down my chest, past my navel, and paused at my firm stomach. I was suddenly awake, aroused near bursting, and almost before she touched me, I reached orgasm. My shame returned.

"Don't worry," she repeated, cleaning me with the towel and wash basin that was on the bed stand. "I will take care of you. Rest now."

Maria lay next to me, young, soft, naked and undemanding. I let spent sexual energy and the weight of fatigue carry me into sleep.

I awoke before dawn, disoriented. When I saw a beautiful woman sleeping next to me, I remembered. I have to get out of here, I thought, with sudden urgency. I showered and dressed as quickly as I could. Maria was awake by then and had put her dress back on, a light, paisley print that hit her just above the knees, and clung to her every movement.

"You are a brave man, Giovanni, leaving home and family far behind to fight this cruel war. I will wait for you until the war is over, if you want me. I could love you and make you a very happy man." She gave me a slip of paper with her address on it.

"Maria, I have to go." Alarms were going off in my head. She was beautiful but I did not love her. She said she'd wait for me, but I could die tomorrow. I pressed into her hand a neatly folded bundle of script money. She protested and pushed the money back at me. I explained that this was a gift for her family and thanked her for everything. Finally, she accepted and I quickly exited. I paid at the desk for Rick and Monique's room for the week and returned to explore the wonders of Paris. In three days, I would be back on the front line, and this would be little more than a dream. I hailed a taxi and asked him to take me to the Eiffel Tower. That night I made a long entry in my diary, lest I forget.

Chapter Six

Battle of the Bulge

I returned to Charlie Company after five days in France with my duffel bag loaded with French Cognac, a bottle for each man in my gun crew, and several bottles for Auwen and Verdel. I smuggled it in and the guys drank it under cover, hidden from the officers. The French liqueur was mostly gone in one night. All the guys wanted to know how I liked the French Mademoiselles. I smiled and answered, "ooh la la," without details, but Auwen and Verdel each managed to ask me privately. They got a few sentences out of me about Maria. I was embarrassed. They knew I'd slept with her. After that there were raised eyebrows and crude comments that I did not deny, discuss, or defend.

When I left for Paris my battalion had just moved into Germany. When I returned from Paris, little if no forward movement had been achieved and the 343rd battalion was still mired in the mud. In fact, the battalion traveled a total of 18 miles during the whole month of December. We held our position at Germany's Siegfried line, firing innumerable shells from every size gun at the rows upon rows of concrete spikes that prevented tank movement. We fired at the pillboxes, which were concrete enforced bunkers with massive walls, sometimes 20 feet thick, for German gun emplacements. The line stretched as far as the eye could see, miles and miles of dragon's teeth, buried mines and concrete bunkers. Our shells bounced off the bunkers. We had to call up the 155mm and 240 mm Howitzer guns to blast the pill boxes. Direct hits from our biggest guns were the only effective means of destroying the pill boxes.

Morale was low as we held our position in the stagnant, muddy trenches. We slept in the wretched cold and rain, socked in, with a cloud cover that offered no visibility for air support from the Army Air Force. We were on our own in the mud and rain with very little forward movement.

While we were bivouacked in Buren, Germany, the third week in December, 1944, my mail caught up with me. I got a packet of letters from home, tied with brown twine, and I read them for days, tissue thin pages written on both sides of light green airmail paper. Florence, my older sister, wrote with news of her young married life and the escapades of her show business husband. The other ten letters were from Josephine, my sister who is a few years younger than me. She wrote every night, and mailed it right after, dropping it in the mailbox at the bottom of the hill, no matter how late or dark it was. New Britain was a safe little town. I pictured Jo mailing my letters; I could see her at the green mailbox. It hung on a concrete pole in front of the Photo Shop at the corner of Glenn and Webster Hill. I read one of Josephine's letters. She translated to me for my parents because they did not read English and I did not read Italian.

Dear Johnny, November 29, 1944

    Mama says, who are you kidding Johnny, your last letter sounds like you are on a European vacation instead of risking your life for your country . . . I miss you terribly and worry and pray for you everyday, dear brother, Mama says she had another dream and is very sad. She knows you will not be home for Christmas as you had planned when General Patton took over in the summer. I saw him on a newsreel and he is quite an impressive General, so tall and tough . . . guess what? I saw my boyfriend, Gary, on a newsreel at the movies! I stood up and yelled, "There's my Gary!" right in the movie house. Can you believe it? . . . but please believe that Mama goes every morning to either St. Peter's or St. Joseph's Church to pray for your safe return, as religiously as I write to you every night before I go to sleep.

All my love,
Josephine

Josephine shared the Gary sighting to cheer me up, but she did not tell me that Gary, her boyfriend, was killed in action in the ETO (European Theater of Operations), six months before the war ended. She'd gotten the news from his mother, a few weeks after she wrote this letter. Josephine took great care in what she wrote to me. This was going to be my third Christmas away from home, one in boot camp, one in Wales, and now it looked like another in Germany. That day, I picked up a stubby, dark green #2 pencil, sharpened it with my knife, and pulled the diary out of my left breast pocket. My hands were cold, almost numb, but that didn't stop me. I made an entry for the day:

Dec. 21, 1944 Buren, Germany, 1500

I miss home more than I can say. Another Christmas away from Mama and her lasagna and custard pie. It is cold and we are stuck here, on rest detail. I don't want to stay here and rest, no matter how tired I am, I want to fight and go home.

We have occupied some deserted homes here in Buren, no heat, can't give away our position. At least I have a roof over me to protect me from the wind and icy snow.

I pulled out the New Testament that had been issued to me by the Army in August, 1943 and read the selection for the day, the story of the Samaritan Woman, John 4: 4-19. Then I wrote a letter home.

Dearest Mama and Papa, December 21, 1944

I cannot tell you how your letters lifted my spirits. Hi Jo. Thank you for your prayers, Mama. Papa, I miss you and often think of your WWI stories and miss how you used to read to me from the history books. Give Vinny a hug for me and if you see Flo tell her I got her letter and will answer soon. Letters from home are like water to a man in the desert, they sustain me, along with my faith and all your prayers. Willie says, "Hi, and pray for me too."

Jesus said, "Everyone who drinks of this water will thirst again. He, however, who drinks of the water that I will give him shall become in him a fountain of water, spring up unto life everlasting." (John 4:4-19).

Mama, don't worry, I am fine, we are at a rest camp, getting hot meals whenever the service battery mess kitchen can bring them up, and we are doing maintenance on the gun. I even saw a movie the other night, a musical with Don Ameche and Betty Grable and her million dollar legs, ohh la la. It was in color. You may have seen it, "Moon over Miami." While the film lasted, I let myself get lost at the movies, just like at home.

All my love,
Johnny

The next day, December 22, we fired rounds from the gun as ordered. H & I firing we called it, Harassment and Interdiction. We were countering the German artillery, hoping to keep them off balance, firing down a corridor which had become known as the "Bowling Alley." We called it that because the Saarlautern River Valley Basin was a long and narrow depression, a strategic strip of land between Germany and France. When our shells exploded in this valley, they reverberated, rumbled, magnified in sound until the boom was thrown back at us, as if we had just bowled a strike in a war zone bowling alley.

Later that day we received march orders to move back into France at Waldweise. No one in Charlie Company knew why we were backtracking after we'd fought so hard to get into Germany. It was cold and we were miserable, getting farther away from ending the war every day, or so it seemed. "What the hell is going on?" asked George Verdel. "What are these cocksuckers doing to us now?"

I didn't have the answer and said nothing.

So I celebrated Christmas, 1944 in Waldweise, France, if you can call it celebrating. We did have church service between strafing from enemy planes. During service, the chaplain, who was Catholic, read, "And she gave birth to her first-born son and wrapped him in swaddling clothes and laid him in a manger, because there was no place for them in the inn" (Luke 2:7).

I missed my family in Connecticut terribly, as they celebrated Christ's birth without me. My gun crew had a nice present for the Germans though: a new Pozit fuse. On Christmas Day, we fired four rounds of TOT's, Timed On Targets, a prearranged and limited firing pattern. The Pozit fuse was a shell that had a timer that we set so that it exploded before impact, right above the heads of the enemy, raining down shrapnel from the heavens. When used in forested areas, the Pozit fuse was set to explode in the treetops, and flaming tree branches would careen through the air, as deadly as any shrapnel.

The Army service kitchen did their best, however, to get us through Christmas, and they could do wonders. On Christmas day, they brought dinner up in huge pots, piping hot, exquisitely cooked, no holds barred for the holidays. The smell of turkey, ham, sweet potatoes, dressing, mashed potatoes, gravy, cranberry sauce, corn, carrots, coffee, pumpkin pie, spiced just right, was almost too good to be true. I was salivating. We were in line to eat but had to wash our mess gear first, which conveniently opened up with a spoon, knife, fork, cup, and plate, still hooked together as one unit. The mess kitchen brought up three 30-gallon galvanized metal pails, set out on the ground, one filled with extremely hot, soapy water, the second with hot disinfectant water, and third for the final hot rinse. We knew the routine, SOP, Standard Operating Procedure, and we quickly moved through the line. One of the guys ahead of me let out a yell. "Holy shit, do you see what's in here, guys? It's a fucking Kraut leg, with the goddamn boot still on!"

First Lieutenant Lubinski came forward, and used a hook to pull out the German boot with the leg severed just above the knee. He threw it into the field. He ordered the pail to be dumped, and the nearest soldier tossed the water, a good ten yards away. We let the Private back into line. One of the Staff Sergeants, Michael Calo, a good guy from my home state of Connecticut, brought in a new pail. I don't think anyone lost their appetite. I know I didn't. Lubinski ordered a couple of GI's to dig a hole and they buried the leg.

1944 turned into 1945. One of our Anti-Aircraft companies, Undo Able, shot down three enemy aircraft to start the New Year right. When word of this passed down the line and reached my company, we all cheered. The mess kitchen served up another heroic turkey dinner, although nothing could compare with Mama's pizza and Italian pastries. I dreamt of her cannoli.

We received orders on the night of January 5th, "Be prepared for movement." The 90th Division, which included my 343rd Field Artillery Battation, prepared, but the march orders were cloaked in such secrecy that it would be hard to prove it. "Blackout Orders" and "Secret Mission" was all that came to us in the scuttlebutt. I made an entry in my diary:

Jan 6, 1945 Waldweise, France 0800

> 94th Division moves in to take our place, takes our call signs, radio frequencies. Vehicle bumpers and shoulder patches blacked. No one knows where we're going. The weather is too cold for words, freezing winds whip the snow into drifts that obscure the roads, roads that are covered in ice, it is well below zero, can't write anymore.

"This man's Army won't tell us where we're going, cocksuckers might as well tell us we're going to hell," was George Verdel's read on the situation.

I can't say I disagreed with him. I never could figure why they went to all the trouble of switching our 90th Division with the 94th Division instead of just sending the 94th to the Bulge. Maybe they thought, as seasoned troops, we were experienced and fresh from our holding mission in Buren, Germany. The truth was we were bone tired.

On January 6th, the 90th Division, as part of III Corps, moved out, on our highly secret, 100 mile trek to Luxembourg, going back over ground we'd fought so hard for in November. What a waste of young men's lives, I thought.

"'Top Secret' my ass, are these sons of bitches stupid or what?" Verdel asked in his usual, expressionless grumble.

We crossed the Moselle River at Koenigsmacher Bridge. Uneventful, but I couldn't help but remember how hard it had been to get across the first time, at Metz, the river swollen with cold November rains, our engineers building pontoon bridges that the Germans kept blowing up. But this time we were going back over territory that we'd already won. There was no resistance from the Germans—they were fighting on the front. We drove all night, in the back of our truck, a 2-1/2-ton 6x6 U.S. Army GMC. It was sure better than walking, but it was cold. Even with the canvas cover over the back, the wind blew through, like a covered wagon in the wild west, and our butts bounced up and down over each rut in the frozen road, jarring until our bones ached not just from the cold, but from the battering. We sat on wooden benches, facing each other in two rows.

As I looked at Harry Burgam, from Michigan, he began his requisite round of pissing and moaning. He whined, "Why me? I don't deserve to die like this. This goddamn government has no feelings, an old man like me, hell, I need a drink to ease the pain."

I felt like tossing Harry off the back of the truck, but I just ignored him.

I had my own misgivings about our 'secret mission.' We are going in the wrong direction, I thought, nobody knows anything, this cold is going to kill me. Although I kept my thoughts to myself, I couldn't stop shaking, my teeth chattered. We were on the road all night, no chance to sleep, barely time to take a piss.

We drove through Luxembourg City. "Where the hell's Luxembourg?" asked Harry. "Never heard of the joint, them dirty sons of bitches." Harry was not the most educated man on my gun crew.

"What a way to see Europe," I remarked, through chattering teeth. Finally, we stopped in Luxembourg at a deserted farm. We were in Ospern.

The wind kept blowing and made the 6 degrees below zero feel like 26 below. I hopped off the back of the truck. "I can't feel my feet, I can't feel my legs," I gasped. I almost fell over, but Sergeant Auwen grabbed me.

"John," Willie echoed, "I can't feel my feet." He was scared. Traveling in the truck behind me, he jumped out the same time I did. "Do you think they're going to try to amputate?"

We grabbed each other and hopped around like Indians doing a tribal dance, only there was no campfire to stomp around.

"John, we got to start praying our rosaries."

Ernest Fletcher joined our dance, as his truck unloaded behind Willie's. Ernie was from Cortes, Colorado and he was a gunner in Able Company. "The problem is, we don't have the right clothes," Ernie said between chattering teeth. He'd boasted of spending a lot of time on the slopes, skiing in Colorado.

"You got that right, Fletcher," Willie said, his breath coming out in puffs of steam. He also knew about cold winters, having grown up in northern Minnesota.

"What I wouldn't do for a nice winter cabin with a roaring fireplace and someone to snuggle up to and drink hot toddies with," Fletcher said.

"You better snap out of it Ernie, we got work to do," I said, enjoying the banter. It helped to keep us going and even imaginary warmth helped.

As soon as we were off duty, the three of us ducked into the barn. Fletcher went off to one side of the barn to find a buddy from Able Company while Willie and I wrapped in our winter coats and GI wool blankets. We huddled together in the hay, but before we could finish a decade of 'Hail Marys', we'd slipped into fitful sleep.

We slept curled up like lovers for warmth, but it helped little. We were on Blackout Orders, which meant no fire, no hot food, only cold K rations, not even a cigarette. The wind blew through the holes in the walls of the barn, which had been shelled by both sides. After a few hours, we were rudely awakened by shrieks and screams.

"Help! We're surrounded! The Germans!" It was Ernie Fletcher.

I picked up my carbine and pointed, but the enemy turned out to be colder and stiffer than the rest of us. Ernie had been sleeping with his arms wrapped around a dead Kraut, who must have been wounded and taken refuge in the barn before we got there. We threw the dead man out in the snow and tried to go back to sleep. We rode Fletcher about this for a long time after. The moment of grotesque levity had lifted our spirits, and not much else did in the days to follow.

Back on the road, we were headed for what would soon be known as "The Battle of the Bulge" by American Army historians, or "The Ardennes Campaign" by Winston Churchill and his chroniclers. We drove towards the stalemated 35th and 26th Divisions. I told myself, I'm going to keep my spirits up so that I can go home. I prayed to the Blessed Virgin Mary every day and promised to make a pilgrimage to the Shrine of the Blessed Virgin in Rome, if I survived the war. I can't explain how my company survived the brutality, with soldiers killed and wounded all around me, except to say my prayers were answered. I made the pilgrimage in 1950.

Verdel read in *Stars and Stripes* that our battalion was entertained by Marlene Dietrich. "Those cocksucking bastards," he said as he grabbed his crotch, "son of a bitch, there's no entertainment here." His grey-blue eyes were old man's eyes. He had a pasty complexion, and his glasses kept falling down his nose. His hair was pale blonde, and his lips curled into a snarl when he spoke, revealing bad teeth, some capped in gold, some replaced by a loose partial bridge. He would adjust his bridge with a forceful thumb push and the resulting click was one of Verdel's characteristic punctuations, along with "son of a bitch."

We moved north to Mecher after crossing the Sure River, a tributary of the Moselle. Although the river appeared to be frozen, our engineers put down pontoon bridges, and we drove across. Our trucks were heavy enough to break through the ice, not to mention the tanks and other heavy equipment. We received our first fire mission orders since we'd been on March Order. I fought the cold and managed to sharpen and grip my pencil somehow to write this in my diary:

Jan. 8, 1945 Mecher, Germany 1500

It is 10 below zero, the snow is at least 18 inches deep.

Our first fire mission since Blackout orders.

Blackout orders meant not only were all the identifying insignia blacked out on our trucks, equipment, and uniforms, but we drove without lights, even at night. There were little blue slits of light on the vehicles where the headlights and tail-lights would normally shine, just bright enough to follow in the dark, to see from a few feet away so that we could convoy at night. Blackout orders meant no fires, not even a match. I am glad I didn't smoke, the guys who would sneak a cigarette better be glad they weren't caught. This was serious business. Our first fire mission meant that we had arrived and we would be making noise. The Krauts were about to feel the force of our artillery.

The first attack was launched on Jan. 9, we fired at least 600 rounds that first day, and I would stroke the barrel of the Howitzer with my gloved hand to keep my hands from freezing. If I kept moving, I could fight the cold. I was Johnny hustle. Soon we'd fired all the shells that had been prepared and stacked the night before. I helped knock the shells out of the boxes and inserted the shells into the casings with one powder bag per mile. I took turns loading the shell into the breach block. Sgt. Auwen relayed co-ordinates to Verdel, our gunner Corporal. Verdel sighted the gun and closed the block. He'd yell "Fire" as he pulled the lanyard cord, and we'd cover our ears, or stuff cotton in them. I have a ringing in my ears, to this day, from being so close to so many discharged artillery shells. The gun would recoil into the spikes, the sighting was corrected if necessary to account for recoil, although this frozen ground did not give much. The process started all over, encase, load, site, and fire.

I wrote in my diary:

Jan. 10, 1945 Mecher, Germany

Artillery barrage successful, skuttlebutt has it that two regiments of infantry jumped off yesterday, with one in reserve. It is so cold, so much ice and snow, rough going, God save the dough boys.

Blessed Virgin Mary, thank you for keeping me out of the infantry, Jesus, Son of God, protect us in this unholy war. God the Father, Son and Holy Ghost, watch over us, I prayed. It seemed like once we started, the fire missions never stopped. Hey Amigo made long hauls in the truck for ammunition, the gun barrel of the 105 Howitzer gave off a lot of heat, felt like it kept us alive as we fired, night and day.

From Mecher we moved to Tarchamps, still in Luxembourg. When we jumped off the truck to position the Howitzer, the snow came up to our knees. The boughs of the pine trees bent under the weight of snow. We were moving towards Bras, Belgium. The 90th Division was supposed to take the high ground and open up the road. Our fire mission at Tarchamps was successful, and the 90th Division moved into Belgium and occupied another firing position at Warden. Our artillery barrage met little resistance. The Germans were surprised. They did not expect a Division of the American Army to attack from the south. We were part of the attack on the German's southern flank of what was to be the final push of the Wehrmacht, the German Army. We capitalized on the lack of resistance, and moved northeast, back into Luxembourg at Allerborn. It seemed that the only way not to freeze to death was to keep moving, keep firing. I wrote in my diary:

Jan. 15, 1945 Warden, Luxembourg, 1530

We visited Belgium today, we're right on the border.
Moved north and Sgt. Auwen tells us we're back in Luxembourg.
Caught the Krauts flatfooted, they're falling back in confusion, we
have to push on, keep the advantage. I'm punchy from no sleep.
German resistance getting weaker, no wonder, we fired 800 rounds
yesterday.

As my battalion moved through Luxembourg, we stopped for fire missions at villages and small towns with names like Wincrange, Stockem, Asselborn, Binsfeld, Weiswampach, Leithum, and Beiler. The locals came out from their villages and lined the roads as we drove by. They offered us food. I grabbed a loaf of bread. It was hard and brown, but a welcome change from our K-ration crackers. I threw a couple of cans of "K's" to the locals in exchange. The women tossed little evergreen wreaths to us, decorated with pine cones. Considering that Luxembourg is the size of Rhode Island, we did a lot of firing in that country, chasing the Krauts back into the Fatherland.

I made another diary entry:

Jan.18, 1945 Weiswampach, Luxembourg 1300

At 0900 yesterday, we prepared a TOT fire mission with 14
other battalions. These Corps attacks are deafening. We fired

at 1030 and again at 1300. German Nebel-werfers were part of the counter attack, the "screaming meemies" are the worst. The six-barrel gun with its high velocity rockets comes in screaming. I hate that gun.

Another diary entry read:

Jan. 24, 1945 Binsfield, Luxembourgh 1600

357 Infantry Regiment occupied the town of Binsfield this morning. German artillery counter-attacked. Our fire mission was to take out the German guns and we fired 900 rounds in two hours. As we drove through Binsfield this afternoon, all that was left of the Germans was blood-stained snow. There is a ringing in my ears, I should be deaf after the Corps attack on Jan. 18th.

At Beiler, we prepared to cross the Our River, which would bring us back into Germany. Our engineers had to construct another pontoon bridge for the heavy equipment and we were waiting for fire mission orders. The infantry moved back and forth in front of us. The previous day, their attempt to cross had been repulsed by German artillery. Germans would not make it easy to cross into the Fatherland. They had a good vantage point on the other side of the river, up on a hill. Also, the deep snow and steep banks of the river made it hard for the infantry to get a footing. The weather was bleak, overcast and gray, poor visibility. To pass the time, we turned to skuttlebutt, and a Private, I think his name was Hank, from the 357th Infantry Regiment, I Company, told us a story.

The day before, while they were trying to cross the river, General Patton approached Hank's regiment. Patton demanded, "Where's the Officer in Charge?" Bullets were whizzing by the General's helmet, and he acted as if he didn't notice, he stood up tall. The rest of the men in the outfit were hitting the ground, looking for any kind of cover.

"I want to speak with the Commanding Officer," Patton demanded. The Captain was nowhere to be found, but the message was quickly passed down the line. Soon the regiment's unshaven officer with no identification of rank on his uniform appeared in front of General Patton.

"Where's your goddamn bars? Your fucking ass belongs up here, and get that ugly beard off your face. Officers in my Army are up front, leading the attack, not directing it from the rear." Patton glared at his Captain and continued, "I will not tolerate cowards in the 3rd Army, and I will see your ass up here where it belongs when I return, Captain, or goddamn it, you'll be one unlucky son of a bitch, debarred and court-martialed."

This display of bravado made quite an impression on the dogfaced dough boys, and sure enough, the next morning, Patton was back to see his Captain, who was a man transformed.

Patton must have brought some luck with him. Or maybe it was like in the movie, where George C. Scott won on Oscar for his portrayal of Patton, who during the Battle of the Bulge, had a chaplain write a very effective prayer for good weather. The fog lifted and skies cleared at the end of the third week in January, long enough for the AAF (Army Air Force) to do some serious bombing. We heard and felt the air strikes. Looking skyward, we saw the bomber formations, accompanied by fighter planes. Once again, head lifted and looking skyward, I wished I was a fighter pilot. What a relief it was to feel the ground rumble beneath our feet, against our backs as we crouched in our foxhole. The drone of the B-17's, as they flew in and dropped 1000 pound bombs, was music to my ears. We felt the impact, living out in the elements the way we were. We saw craters the size of a football field blown into the frozen ground. After the Flying Fortresses had dropped their bombs, we saw hundreds of dead Germans for miles around. The bomb concussion alone was enough to kill you. Little towns that took direct hits were leveled.

Once we made it across the Our River, on January 29th, we heard another story from a member of the infantry, this time it was a dough boy from Company L, 357th Regiment. His company was ready to cross the river and were told to do it right—there were Generals watching on the other side, shooting film for a newsreel. Captain Colby ordered one of his Lieutenants, "Take that house." They were going to use it as a shield to fire on German resistance. The Officer was new to the outfit, a replacement. He knocked on the door, told the Germans to surrender, and they did. In this manner, the Americans took 100 prisoners that day, before crossing into Germany. I guess this group of Germans was more tired of the war than we were, having fought in Europe for six years to our one. They'd been in retreat before the 90th Division and were about to get pushed back into the Fatherland. The Our River is a border between Germany and Belgium. The Generals, however, did not approve of this unorthodox method of war, and the newsreel never made it for public viewing.

We crossed into Germany and our first position was at Winterspelt. We did not have fire orders, and had dug our trenches in a snow-covered forest. Lt. Lubinski gave us another pep talk, "Heads up men, we are back in Germany. General Patton's orders are to keep your feet warm and your socks dry. Trench foot is not a ticket home. It is an offense punishable by court-martial."

"Fuck you Frank," came in a chorus from my company, almost before Lubinski was out of earshot. There was no way to keep our feet warm and dry, we had no fires, it was zero or below, we were sleeping in holes in the ground, in the snow, eating chunks of frozen cheese from cans of "K" rations.

It is a miracle that I did not get frostbite. I was careful with my feet. I moved around as much as possible to encourage circulation, I wrapped my legs and feet in wool blankets whenever I could. Very rarely we would take our socks and shoes off and massage our feet until circulation returned.

Night fell early in the dismal northland in the winter months, around 1700. On this night, the moon rose at sunset and illuminated a row of Norway Spruce, their branches heavy with ice and snow. I was on guard duty with Big Jim, the Indian. Suddenly, I saw ghostly figures coming out of the woods, moving towards us. We held our fire, and I slipped out of the trench to alert the Corporal of the guards. I told Jim, "Don't fire, it will give away our position."

We aimed our 50 caliber machine guns and our carbines at the approaching soldiers. As they got closer, we saw one of them was holding a white flag, he spoke English with a thick, guttural accent, and repeated frantically, "Achten, Achten, don't shoot, don't shoot."

They marched in single file in three lines, hands up in the air. I stayed on my gun, ready to attack. This could be a trick. Captain Bremer, the Commander of "C" Battery, instructed some of our men, who spoke German, to talk to the soldiers. The Germans had been separated from their outfits, after the AAF air strikes, with no food, no ammo. They were ready to surrender. At least 100 Germans surrendered that night, a silent night on the front. Since we didn't have a fire mission, our job was to guard this position, a small clearing in the woods on a beautiful moonlit night. The spruce and fir trees were laden with snow, a pristine scene, like one reproduced on a Currier and Ives's Christmas card, mailed all over the world, carrying wishes for joy and peace. It was hard to believe that such beauty still existed in war-torn Europe, but we were still freezing cold and sleep deprived. Everything took on a surrealistic shimmer, the night, the Germans who moved like ghosts and materialized out of the woods.

I wrote in my diary:

Feb. 2, 1945 Winterspelt, Germany 0900

How many times are we going to cross into Germany? I am cold, hungry and tired of this war. Division keeps going east, a nightmare, it's like we are back at the Siegfried line. Last night the Germans came out of the woods like ghosts, to surrender. I almost shot them. Strange things happen to me on guard duty. PFC Slade from Charlie Company did some translating for the Germans and confirmed what we already knew. Many of the Germans would rather be captured by Americans, brought behind the front line, and treated fairly. They feet the war is lost, now that we have collapsed "The Bulge." None of them want to be captured by the Russians, whose reputation is ruthless. Not to mention what the Nazi's did when they invaded Russia. Americans have a reputation for honoring the Geneva Convention when dealing with prisoners of war.

We occupied four more battalion positions in Germany before we earned a rest, with fire missions at Eigelsheid, Heckhuscheid, Uttfeld, and Lichtenborn. Night and day, we fired the gun. Back in their own country, the Nazi's had their backs against the wall. With their feet on native soil they felt grounded in the Fatherland, and many Germans would fight to the finish, if they were able. Our mission was to keep them on the run. We fired TOT's. Our orders were to remain on the offensive, although we were often under attack, mostly by German machine guns and mortars. Auwen said captured Krauts were feeding us information about German assembly points, and we succeeded in taking out the German light artillery.

When we got to Lichtenborn, Germany, things changed. The ice was turning to mud and the Germans quit firing back. We were sent north to Winterscheid, just inside the German border, close to the Our River. We stayed there for six days. They called it Rest Camp. It was either rest for our company or collapse.

I still don't know how I survived the Battle of the Bulge. There was so much blood spilled in the Ardennes Forest that the snow was red. We were deaf from the constant explosions, round after round of bursting artillery shells lit up the sky at night. As we followed the infantry through the battlefield, through the snow that was more red than white, we saw so many bodies, abandoned in the fields. One time, when our truck was stalled in a convoy, we saw stacks of bodies, American GI's stacked like cordwood stored in a shed, no body bags, no ceremony. The cemetery crews could not keep up, even though they worked as fast as they could to collect the dead. We saw them tossing the frozen stiffs on the back of their trucks, and the bodies hit with a sickening thump. At night we huddled together to grab moments of broken sleep, wrapped in all our clothes and covered in our olive drab blankets, but there was very little warmth.

Unlike summer in France, there was no stench. When our truck drove past what was left of the dead, the German and American soldiers were frozen and crumpled with open gaping wounds. This was brutal winter combat. I have never been so cold, hungry, tired, and deprived before or since. Fortunately, this late in the war, I had become conditioned to these horrible scenes of death passing before me and in order to survive, I became numb to it.

Looking back through my book, Mission Accomplished, 343rd F.A.BN, printed by the Army in Germany, November, 1945 and given to me upon discharge, I found a page of statistics. During the Battle of the Bulge, my battalion fired 37,869 rounds of ammunition. My Howitzer was one of many, but no matter how this number is divided up, that was the most rounds of ammunition fired by my battalion during any campaign of WWII. The 343rd participated in 772 fire missions between Jan. 8 and Feb. 22, 1945. This frenetic activity and astounding number of rounds fired must be the reason I survived. I kept moving to the rhythm of the gun, "encase, load, site, fire" and "encase, load, site, fire."

When Patton ordered us out of Germany, back through France and into Luxembourg, we did not know what was going on, but we knew how to follow orders, no matter how much griping and moaning we did. The fact that the Germans mounted a major winter offensive when the weather was terrible and supplies were minimal was nearly unprecedented. Frederick the Great had done it when he was King of Prussia in the 1700's, but General Patton was probably one of the few leaders who could pull that fact out of the hat. Just as improbable was our ability to be pulled off the line in winter where we were involved in an eastward attack at the front, turn around 90 degrees, travel 100 miles without sleep, winter boots, or source of heat, and attack the southern flank of the German offensive.

After we dissolved the "Bulge," my outfit returned to Germany and kept the Wehrmacht on the run, until we finally got a break. When we heard that billets had been arranged for us in Winterscheid, Germany, we could not have been more ready for a hot meal, a shower, clean clothes, and a cot to sleep in under tent cover. The weather was overcast, there was rain and mud. No one cared. We weren't sleeping out in slit trenches covered in mud. Let it rain.

We even saw a movie, Lost in a Harem, with Abbott & Costello. They had us laughing like kids with its silly plot twists and sidesplitting gags. Abbot and Costello played Pete and Harvey, two American magicians stranded in an Arabian Nights kingdom. Willie and I laughed so hard during their burlesque routine, "Slowly I Turned," that for an hour and a half we nearly forgot the war.

Mail call caught up with me again, and I untied my bundle of light green letters written in Josephine's careful hand, routed through the Army Post Office, A.P.O., in New York, a red six cent airmail stamp affixed to each one. I knew I was blessed. I felt the love and concern radiating through the letters even before I read them.

Dearest Johnny, January 25, 1945

Have received two letters from you dated in Dec. but nothing recently and Mama is praying hard for you, and Papa worries about you out in the European winter. . . . Please write and let us know that you are okay . . . We read in the paper that the Allies are winning decisive battles in the ETO. Mama tells Papa not to worry, she feels that you are safe . . . Mama dreamt that you were home in your bed, sleeping like a baby, while she is cooking your favorite spaghetti dish with garlic bread. She says that is a good sign . . .

> With all my love, all my life,
> Josephine

From February 25 to March 3, 1945, we rested, enjoying every mouthful of hot food, every minute of hot shower and piece of clean clothing. I prayed every day in thankfulness for my survival, to God, the Father in heaven, and to Mary, Mother of God, for watching over me and to Jesus, Son of God, for saving me with his death on the cross. I read my daily prayers with Willie, and we prayed the rosary together, "Glory be to the Father, to the Son and to the Holy Ghost, as it was in the beginning is now and ever shall be."

The reading for Feb. 28th was from Matthew 8:19-20. ". . . a Scribe came and said to him, 'Master, I will follow thee wherever thou goest.'" But Jesus said to him, "The foxes have dens, and the birds of the air have nests; but the Son of Man has nowhere to lay his head."

Before I went to sleep, I wrote in my diary, trying not to be overly optimistic. The Germans had a way of bouncing back, as I had seen three times before, but I did write an optimistic letter home to the family in Connecticut.

Chapter Seven

The Battle of Germany, VE Day

We left rest camp at Wintersheid and the next day I made a diary entry:

March 4, 1945 Nieder Hersdorf, Germany 1700

> Yesterday we crossed the Prum River and had the guns and ourselves dug in by 2300, our position was near Winregen. Today we moved to Nieder Hersdorf and fired nearly 500 rounds. We have new march orders to move to Kopp. Infantry meeting resistance at the Kyll River from the high ground of the eastern banks, the Heinie side. The infantry calls it Little Siegfried because of the German gun emplacements. The Krauts destroy every bridge when they retreat. They destroy Germany before we can move forward, blowing up their own country while we fight in the rain and mud. General Mud, the German's best defense, but everyone's enemy. Time to go, we have another fire mission at 1800.

We were in the middle of the spring thaw. For three months we'd been freezing and fighting in the ice and snow, but now the snow had melted and the ground turned to muck. The roads could not support the parade of heavy equipment brought in by the American Army. The sides of the unpaved roads crumbled and disappeared into a field of mud as the rains came down and the weather stayed well above freezing. We were on our way to the Kyll River after crossing the Prum, and mud was even worse in river valleys.

Sgt. Auwen yelled, "Everyone off the truck, we aren't going anywhere. Goddamn it, we need a mother fucking tank to pull us out."

Hey Amigo had tried to use the winch on the front of the truck to free our 2 ½ ton GMC. We'd hooked the cable up to a tree and he had engaged the motorized crank but the six wheels were more than half submerged. There was no traction, even though the truck had six wheel drive and six on the floor. A column of trucks backed up behind us while off road tanks lumbered methodically forward. Tanks moved on tracks that were oblivious to dissolved roadways and inclement weather.

Sgt. Auwen barked out orders, "Varano, you and Verdel get your asses over here, cut some logs and wedge them under the back tires."

The mud sucked on my boots when I hopped off the back. I took an ax from the side rack where it was attached to the outside of the truck and so did Verdel. We trudged off into a grove of trees beside the muddy mess that used to be a dirt road and continued our conversation.

"Why do you think we hardly see *Stars and Stripes*?" Verdel grumbled.

"The mail truck is probably stuck in the mud," I answered.

"Ah, c'mon Johnny, it's a daily newspaper, they could air drop it with supplies."

I selected a small tree and took a swing. Verdel, a few yards away, was doing the same thing. We fell into a wood-chopping rhythm.

"Patton is always in the headlines," I said, "why would he keep us from reading *Stars and Stripes*?"

"Hell, Johnny, Patton's pissed. The cocksucker tried to kick out the reporters from his headquarters. He tried to get Mauldin fired."

I remembered the scuttlebutt. Maybe Verdel was right. There had been a lot of talk about how mad Patton was when he found reporters eating in Officers' Mess. And as much as we loved Bill Mauldin's irreverent cartoons starring the infantry dogfaces, Willie and Joe, we'd heard that Patton hated them.

"Okay, so he's an arrogant S.O.B.," I admitted, "but he's our General and the Germans are on the run. You got to give him points for that, George."

We stopped chopping and both moved to the other side of our selected trees. We'd been together night and day for so long that we were like two cogs in the same wheel.

Verdel lost interest in arguing and said, "Remember that cartoon that really pissed him off?" He described the one by Mauldin of two Generals at a beautiful mountain lookout.

We both started laughing and I said, "Yeah, the one that read, 'Beautiful view. Is there one for the enlisted men?'"

We laughed until we felled our young trees. We set to whacking off branches and chopping the trunk into small logs.

"Yeah, that's the one, Patton tries to fire Mauldin and Ike says, 'Screw you George, the men need some laughs,'" Verdel added.

"All rumor and scuttlebutt," I said to Verdel, but I thought he was right. Josephine had sent me a newspaper clipping from home. Patton's demand to have the cartoonist, Bill Mauldin, fired had even turned into a big story in the civilian newspapers.

"I hate Patton," Verdel said, "he thinks his shit doesn't stink."

"Geeze, Verdel, you know the more headlines Patton gets, the better he performs. Don't you want to get out of this mud, beat the Germans, and get back home?"

"You got that right, Johnny," Verdel concluded, and we hauled the logs over to the truck and shoved them against the tires.

A few days later, I made a short diary entry:

March 6, 1945 Kyll River, Germany 2200

> We fired all day yesterday and through most of the previous night to secure the bridgehead.

Yesterday evening the infantry forded the Kyll.

We were on the move, it felt like the Wehrmacht was in retreat, and this was the pervasive feeling in the next entry I made:

March 10, 1945 Mayen, Germany 0900

> We traveled 40 miles yesterday, the roads cluttered with abandoned German vehicles, entire motor pools, it looked like, by the side of the road, out of gas maybe or the drivers too busy retreating. When we took Mayen, all buildings in town were flying the white flag. The people hung out sheets, pillow cases, aprons, petticoats, every and anything white they could find was flying in the breeze, flapping out of windows. They were tired of fighting. We saw our first jet-propelled planes, German V-3's, they flew over with incredible speed, slowing suddenly to drop their bombs and then streak out of sight, harassing the battalion. By the time we heard their bombs explode, they were long gone, swoosh and boom. Lubinski says they fly 600-700 mph. We got the word that Sgt. Bailey's gun section from 343rd Able Battery fired 10 rounds across the Rhine, the first shells from our Division artillery to go over.

By March 11, we were looking to cross the Moselle River once again, this time at Rubenbach, Germany. It seemed that the Moselle was destined to be the 90th Division's tormentor. We had double-crossed it in France, because of the Battle of the Bulge. Now this blasted river had snaked its way back through Germany. The Moselle was swollen once again due to melting snow and spring rain and we stalled on the bridgeless banks. Orders from Division HQ sent us upstream. I wrote in my diary the next day. I was seeing so much, with my eyes wide open. It hurt but it helped to write it down:

March 12, 1945 Kalt, Germany 1300

Yesterday we advanced upstream, engineers looking for a site to build another pontoon bridge. As we moved into Kalt, houses flew a white flag. Those that didn't were warned and then attacked. If occupants of the houses fired upon us, the buildings were leveled. Movement is slow, as roads are cluttered with shattered vehicles and displaced persons, it is heart-breaking to see. Lines of tattered refugees, men, women and children, French, Poles, Russians, Czechs, Yugoslavs, Dutch, Belgians, British, bedraggled, carrying all their possessions in a little wagon or a rucksack. Some are barefoot, some with wooden shoes, some wearing mismatched articles of stolen uniforms.

The farther we advanced into Germany, the more we encountered columns of refugees; many had been slave laborers for the Germans. They were in such bad shape, uncared for, full of lice, sores, cuts and bruises. There were old people, little kids, men and women stooped under their bundles, or dragging rickety carts behind them. Now I understood why so many of the German shells were duds, why the guns misfired, why their equipment broke down. These forced laborers sabotaged their work in the ammunition plants, the gun factories, and the vehicle manufacturing plants. I wondered how anyone could be treated so badly and still work. Despite the terrible condition the slave laborers had lived in for years, they looked up at us and smiled as we drove by, gratitude in their eyes. We, the Americans, were their liberators. I felt so bad for them, sometimes I had to turn away. We tossed them as many K rations as we could. I looked more closely at the food that we had all grown so tired of, the food provided by the Army that kept us alive. Our K rations came in packages the size of a Cracker Jack box. There were three different kinds. Breakfast K ration included biscuits that were like crackers, a fruit bar wrapped in white wax paper, an egg and meat mixture in a tiny pop-top vacuum sealed can, chewing gum and water purification tablets. Dinner K rations included a can of compressed meat or fish, a packet of crackers and a dense chocolate bar in brown waxed paper. It was made with a lot of flour, I presume, so that the chocolate would not melt, plus an envelope of instant coffee, sugar and cigarettes. The supper K ration included a can of pork, or something that I could barely eat and that we called spam. There were more crackers, candy, bland yellow cheese in a can, an envelope of lemon powder, a wooden spoon, a packet of four named brand cigarettes that included unfiltered Camels, Lucky Strikes or Chesterfields, and matches.

Many of the refugees were too far gone to be helped by K rations, and the Red Cross and our medics did the best they could to supply first aid and hospital care for these victims of war. Three days later, I wrote in my diary once again:

March 15, 1945 Alken, Germany 1500

> Yesterday we started at 0250, and as part of XII Corps attack, we shelled the enemy strong points, at 0500 the infantry crossed the Moselle in assault boats. By 1200 engineers had a bridge across, and at 2200 our battalion was across. We dug in the gun 50 yards from the river, worked under artificial moonlight. It was the strangest thing, the night was cloudy, and the searchlight unit, far in the rear, turned three powerful spotlights up toward the heavens. The light bounced off the clouds, illuminated the night around us with a dim glow, like moonlight. It made it possible to maneuver 20 hrs. yesterday out of 24. This morning at 0400, German 88's and flak guns attacked the infantry. Our 105's took them out.

Sgt. Auwen had just gotten off the phone with the CP. He told us that bumper to bumper convoys of Germans were stampeding eastward toward the Rhine River. This was according to forward observers flying in Piper Cub planes. Long range artillery from our Division's 345th battalion was laid on the column, that is the 155-mm Howitzers, guns with a good ten-mile range and 100 pound shells. The Piper Cub pilots reported increasing havoc in the German lines, turning the retreat into a rout. The Germans were headed for the security of the Rhine for something like the Nazi's version of Custer's Last Stand or Hitler's rewrite of "Remember the Alamo."

We also headed for the Rhine. To us, it was more than another bridgeless river to cross, and everyone was talking. The consensus was that once we crossed the Rhine, Germany would fall. Three days later, I wrote in my diary:

March 18, 1945 Boppard, Germany 0830

> Yesterday we reached the banks of the Rhine, seven miles below Koblenz. We captured the town of Boppard. We are itching to cross. Today Auwen told us that the 90th Division cleared the west bank of the river from Boppard to Binger. We just got new orders. We are to drive southeast, cross the Nahe River, and capture the city of Mainz.

We grumbled about the change of direction, the change of orders. We arrived outside of Mainz at 1500 on March 22nd, and positioned the gun in a suburb called Marienborn. It had been stop and go along the way, slam on the breaks, pull off the road, fire a few rounds, bang, and then back on the road and go, go, go. The Luftwaffe, or German Air Force, had put in an appearance to remind us that we were in Germany. We saw Messerschmitts and Folke-Wulfs, but we only heard the V-3 jets. Those jets were really something. They were so fast, the Ack-Ack boys couldn't touch them, but our Ack-Ack guns did bring down three German planes.

The city of Mainz surrendered. The citizens were sick of Nazi lies and tired of war, and according to reports from CP, relayed to us by Sgt. Auwen, the citizens led American troops safely through streets and roads that were heavily mined. When our battalion moved through Mainz, we didn't see one building that hadn't been bombed. We saw a lot of badly damaged towns in France, and I thought I knew about destruction, but these towns in Germany had been obliterated. Mainz was mostly rubble because of repeated air attacks. When a city was destroyed by high explosives from tons of Air Force bomb drops, the destruction went deep, into sewer systems, water mains, electrical conduits. We were scheduled to stop for a few days in Marienborn, so plans were made to clean up, the guns, ourselves, and our laundry. We needed to get the mud off and eat hot meals.

At 0500 on March 23, Sgt. Auwen announced, "New orders, hitch up the gun, stow your gear, get your ass moving, we march at 0600. No rest for you mother-fuckers, we're heading for the Rhine, goddamn it."

This was a rude awakening for me and Stud. We'd just gotten off guard duty at 0500. "Geeze, Johnny, I was looking forward to a hot shower," Stud said to me, half awake, as we scrambled out of our slit trench, one that we'd dug just the night before, as deep and long as we could manage, figuring to be here until Palm Sunday.

"You got that right Stud, I thought the chaplain would catch up to us for Sunday mass. You know it's only ten days until Easter," I said, as we both helped Verdel remove the camouflage net from over the Howitzer.

Stud had replaced Big Jim, my usual trench partner. Jim had been taken to the infirmary a week earlier, while the rest of us marched through the mud between the Moselle and the Rhine rivers. Jim had a severe case of dysentery. He was too weak to stand much less fire the gun. Stud transferred over from another gun in "C" Battery. The guys in my company knew him and liked him. His real name was William Clayton, from St. Louis, Missouri. "Stud" was short for "Stud Horse" because the man was well hung. I could not give an eye witness account, but Stud's ample endowment was accepted as fact among the guys.

We moved the 30 miles or so with the 357th Infantry and, together, our Combat Team arrived at Oppenheim with orders to expand the bridgehead at the Rhine. We did some serious firing and sent round after round across the river. Patton's 5th Infantry Division had already crossed, and we were hitting the Germans with shell after shell, "firing for effect," as requested by the infantry on the other side.

Our orders were to wait for the 89th Infantry Division, but they were having some kind of traffic jam. Sgt. Auwen came up to us and announced, "New orders, we are going across."

That evening, on March 23, 1945, the 343rd FABn rumbled across the pontoon bridge. We were the first artillery unit in the 3rd Army to cross the Rhine. We did it in 12 minutes and moved into position at Leeheim, just before 8 pm or 2000 hours.

Sgt. Auwen had us dig in the gun, then we dug our trenches and got our fire orders. The 357th had crossed before us, made contact with the enemy, and we fired well into the night. I am amazed to think how easily I lifted those 33-pound shells, 105mm in diameter, and loaded them into the breech as we fired again and again. We could feel victory; we were in the final stages. There was no stopping us now. We had seen the Prisoner of War cages bulging with Germans, captured or surrendered. They too wanted to be done with this war. Finally a little before midnight, at 2350, it was my turn to rest.

As soon as Stud and I had settled into our trench, we heard the distinctive drone of German planes, and then we were being strafed. Jesus, Mary and Joseph, I just needed a few hours sleep. We shrunk down under our helmets and heard an explosion right above us. It was a shell from one of our Ack-Ack guns. At least it was friendly fire, but way too close.

Stud turned to me with his gentle Midwestern drawl, "John, I'm hit."

"I don't see anything, Stud," I tried to assure him. It was too dark for me to see anything, but then he started to moan. I thought of his family back home. I put my arm around his shoulders and stopped when I felt something warm and wet between his shoulder blades. I slowly pulled my hand back covered with his blood and tried not to frighten him.

"Yeah, you're hit, Stud. It's not bad," I lied. I did not want to increase his heart rate, but even in the darkness I could feel that it was a serious wound, and that he was bleeding profusely. He must have been hit by a red-hot piece of shrapnel from our own Ack-Acks.

"Stay quiet, I'll be right back," I told him and crawled out of the trench to find Verdel, the senior member of our gun crew.

"Hey, George, Stud's hit. It looks bad."

George got on the horn, a portable telephone used to communicate with the CP. The medics came and carried Stud out on a stretcher, lying on his stomach. They poured sulfur powder into the wound to stop the bleeding and prevent infection. Stud was brought to the field hospital. I was really shook up. We had been celebrating a few hours earlier that the war would soon be over. It was spring, and Stud and I had dug a trench just big enough and barely deep enough for the two of us, so that moving took well-timed cooperation. It had gone something like this.

"Hey Stud, my arm's asleep, let's turn," I'd say.

"Okay, Johnny, one, two, three, go," and we'd turn in unison.

We were inches apart when he got hit. I'd known Stud since I'd joined the 343rd, he was a fellow cannoneer in Charlie Battery. I felt like I knew his wife, Maureen, too. For months I had been reading her letters aloud to Stud and writing her back as he dictated. Stud was illiterate, but that made him no less likeable. He was good-natured, a good soldier. I prayed for him during the few hours of darkness that remained, and in between I had a short and fitful sleep.

Word came back from Battalion HQ the next day that Stud was going to make it, but he was done with combat. He got his Purple Heart and a ticket home to St. Louis and his wife, Maureen.

I made the following diary entries:

March 25, 1945 Darmstadt, Germany 0900

Since we entered Germany, our company has lost Big Jim to illness and Stud to shrapnel, both my trench mates. We've crossed the Prum, Kyll, Moselle, and the Rhine Rivers so it makes sense that our march orders send us to the Main River, east of Frankfurt. We've encountered strong resistance here at Darmstadt. It's not over yet. I'm going without a fox hole partner for awhile and I am praying a lot.

March 28 Wachembuchen, Germany 1500

At 0330 this morning, infantry forded the Main River five days after crossing the Rhine. Our battalion crossed at 1200. We have new orders now for rest and recuperation. In the last three weeks we have driven hundreds of miles through Germany, captured thousands of prisoners, and killed almost as many. Everywhere now we see white flags. They have replaced the Swastika. Villages and towns display banners of surrender, and we are surprised to be welcomed by the communities. They press food and wine into our hands. Many Germans despised the Nazis and welcome the American invaders, but there is fear behind their eyes—fear of retribution and punishment. It's not the same feeling of jubilation that we experienced when we liberated the French, although we were also foreigners in their country, and freed them from Nazi rule. But the Nazis are the German's own, and even the common people, the civilians, know that they will suffer.

Our rest stop in the vicinity of Hersfeld extended into Holy Thursday, Good Friday, and Holy Saturday. Willie and I met at mail call on Holy Saturday.

"Johnny, I got a letter from my mother," Willie announced, holding the pages he'd just read and grinning. "She says she's praying hard for both of us. Mom and Pop have a map of Germany up on the wall in the den, under the moose head, and they are following our progress. They say we crossed the Rhine River."

"Willie, that's great, they are only a few days behind us, maybe they'll be able to tell where we go next," I laughed.

"Nah, Johnny, you know the censors wouldn't let that get through," Willie replied.

"But if they see it in a newsreel, it shouldn't be censored," I countered.

"Well, the question is, did the ETO see the newsreel," Willie shot back.

Then I opened a letter from home.

Dear Johnny, Sunday, March 18, 1945

We read in the papers that the 90th Division is moving swiftly through Germany. It said that you have crossed the Moselle River and are headed for the Rhine River, even though the Germans blow up everything as they retreat. The paper said your engineers can build a bridge across a river in less than a day. Is that true? Mama and Papa send their love. They are working hard for the war effort. Papa in the Machine parts factory and Mama making shirts in the sewing shop. We all pray it will be over soon.

I took our little brother Vinny to the movies, and as we watched the newsreels he got very excited when he saw some soldiers shooting an artillery gun. We saw General Patton leading his 3rd Army in battle through Germany.

Florence is on the road with husband Al Gentile and his band. They have been doing stateside shows for the USO.

Next Sunday is Palm Sunday, and I know this is your favorite time of year. We are all praying so hard for you this Easter, hoping the war will end and that you will soon be home. I hope you get a good Easter dinner and that the weather has improved.

Love and Prayers,
Josephine

P.S. Enclosed is a note from Vinny.

Dear Brother,

Yesterday I went to the movies with Jo. When I saw a soldier behind a large gun, I hoped it was you. I am ten years old now and you missed my last birthday. I miss you and want you to come home.

Your brother,
Vin

Easter Sunday came on April 1st. We had mass out in a field, there was a chill in the air, mud everywhere, but the sun came out for our General Absolution and Holy Communion. The priest talked about Death and Resurrection and Eternal Life. That is what we need to think about, he said, pray that soon all this killing will come to an end.

I wrote a letter home:

Dear Josephine, Easter Sunday
April 1, 1945, Germany

Mama and Papa, I love you so much, and Vinny, thank you for the letter. Jo, as usual your letters cheered me and brought love and warmth into my heart. Bless you all for your prayers and concern and for working so hard in the war effort back home. We had Easter Mass today followed by Easter dinner, the works, ham, turkey, mashed potatoes and gravy, vegetables and fruit, coffee and pie for desert. A hot meal is a big event here and the funny thing is it makes me miss Mama's cooking even more. I hope your Easter Sunday was a blessed one. The reading at Mass today was so powerful. Willie and I talked about it afterward. Matthew 28:2-6 "And behold, there was a great earthquake: for an angel of the Lord descended from heaven and came and rolled back the stone, and sat upon it. His appearance was like lightning and his raiment white as snow. And for fear of him the guards became like dead men. But the angel said to the women, 'Do not be afraid; for I know that you seek Jesus who was crucified. He is not here; for he has risen.'"

All my love,
Johnny

The next morning we left Hersfeld with march orders at 0800 and moved out toward Zella Mehlis, where we captured a small arms factory. The Germans made excellent handguns, and everyone who wanted one, got one. I acquired a Walther P-38, a handsome little automatic pistol, and Hey Amigo made leather shoulder holsters for everyone in our gun company. Good old Jose Alcorta, a man of many talents, not only a good driver, ace mechanic and relentless provider of ammo, but an excellent leather worker.

That gun, tucked under my left shoulder, was quite handy when I became part of the German occupation forces after VE Day, and also when I returned to Germany in 1950, but that's another story.

We moved through the hills of the Thuringen Forest and headed southeast, and our objective changed once again. Instead of Dresden, we were heading for Prague. It was about this time, the first week in April, that the scuttlebutt in the battalion reached a fevered pitch concerning the discovery of a huge amount of gold and treasures that the Nazis had hidden in the underground tunnels of a salt mine in Merkers. The story went like this:

On April 5, a patrol jeep from the 90th Division was enforcing curfew near Merkers when they stopped a woman for questioning. She said she was a displaced person from France and her friend was close to her time of delivery. She was going to get a German midwife. The American soldiers gave the woman a ride, and checked on her story, which seemed to be true. The GI's waited and gave the two women a ride home during which one of the women pointed out, "There's the entrance to the mine where the Germans buried all the gold."

The 90th Division soldiers told their superiors, and the word was passed up the ranks to the Division Commander, General Herbert L. Earnest. This rumor had been confirmed by other displaced persons and civilians in the area who claimed to be part of the slave labor force used by the Germans to unload and store the gold, as well as other treasures. This information was gathered by the Military Intelligence Team 404-G, a team that had been attached to the 358th Infantry Regiment.

On April 6, General Earnest ordered our own 357th Infantry Regiment to guard all known entrances to the mine, along with the 712th Tank Battalion. The story was getting bigger by the minute. By this time it had been learned that the head cashier of the German Reichsbank was at Merkers. His name was Werner Veick and he indicated, upon questioning, that the entire gold reserve of Berlin's Reichsbank was stored in the mine.

Corps Commander General Manton S. Eddy was informed and he immediately told his Commanding Officer, General George S. Patton. Patton said to keep a lid on it. By April 7, generators had been brought in for power and electricity and Lt. Colonel William A. Russell entered the mine. He was accompanied by Signal Corps photographers, German mining officials and Dr. Paul Rave, a German museum official who said he was at Merkers to protect the art treasures stored in the mine. They went down 2,100 feet, in an elevator, to the bottom of the main shaft. They found 550 bags of Riechsmarks stacked along the walls but a three foot thick brick wall protected the main vault with a steel vault door in the center.

Patton ordered General Eddy to blow the door and the next morning, Army engineers were brought down to the mine, along with photographers, reporters, General Earnest and Colonel Russell. One of the engineers inspected the wall around the vault door and said he could blast through it with ½ stick of dynamite, which he did. The Americans entered the vault, which was 75 feet wide and 150 feet long with 12-foot high ceilings. An inventory was made in the well-lit, poorly ventilated room. There were seven thousand bags laid out in twenty rows stacked knee deep along with over 200 containers of SS loot, valuables stolen by the Nazi Storm Troopers, most likely from the Jews. While the vault was being inventoried, other Americans searched the tunnels and found 2000 famous paintings and hundreds of pieces of sculpture. The salt mine at Merkers contained one hundred tons of gold bullion, five billion German marks, and two million American dollars. General Eddy added the 773rd Tank Destroyer Battalion and numerous anti-aircraft guns to protect the entrances to the mine.

On April 8, Patton learned that the press had found out about the Merkers mine and had published stories. So much for keeping a lid on it. Patton called General Omar N. Bradley, who notified SHAEF, the Supreme Headquarters, Allied Expeditionary Force, commanded by General Dwight D. Eisenhower. Eisenhower sent Colonel Bernard D. Bernstein to take over the Merkers operation. He was in charge of handling foreign funds with the Department of Treasury when he was commissioned a Colonel.

Bernstein toured the mine on April 10th and then drove to Patton's headquarters. Patton told Bernstein he was glad to have Eisenhower take responsibility for the gold and Bernstein told him they had to move it as quickly as possible to Frankfurt. Under the Big Three arrangements at Yalta, the Russians would take over the Merkers part of Germany as soon as the war ended, which could be very soon. Patton was astounded, he did not know about that provision of the Yalta agreement.

Since one of our infantry battalions and one of our tank battalions was guarding the gold, everyone in our gun company had opinions about the Merkers mine treasure. Auwen said, "You know those lucky assholes are stealing gold bars to have a stash of cash after the war."

"Sure," Verdel grumbled, "all you do is sneak it out, bury it, come back after the dust settles, and you're one lucky son of a bitch."

On April 12, Generals Eisenhower, Bradley and Patton inspected the mine along with Brigadier General Otto O. Weyland. It has been reported, that as the shaky elevator descended with increasing speed down into the pitch-black shaft on a single cable, Patton noted that if the cable snapped "promotions in the United States Army would be considerably stimulated," to which Eisenhower responded, "OK George, that's enough, no more cracks until we are above ground again."

It has also been reported that near the end of the inspection Bradley turned to Patton and said, "If these were the old free-booting days when a soldier kept his loot, you'd be the richest man in the world," to which Patton smiled and said nothing.

We'd heard that Patton wanted to keep the gold in the mine a secret and make a gold medallion out of some of it for every "son of a bitch in the Third Army." We also heard he was going to hide the rest of it until peacetime, when the military budget was next to nothing, and use it to make new weapons to fight the Russians.

The gold found in the mine was truly the dragon's hoard of the Nazi Regime, representing 91% of the gold found in Germany and inventoried at Frankfurt after the war ended. Being from a civilized country, the Americans did not consider it war booty, but we could not even imagine what the Russians would have done with the discovery. Considering that it almost fell into Russian hands, we couldn't help but wonder why the Germans would hide in one spot nearly all the Nazi gold reserves plus gold looted from many central banks in Europe.

The story continued to unravel. It seemed to be all we talked about in early April, 1945. It was in the newspapers back home, in *Stars and Stripes*, and the hot topic on the scuttlebutt circuit. One thing we did know was that on February 3rd, 1945, the Eighth Air Force sent over more than 900 B-17 bombers to partake in a concerted air strike over Berlin, Germany's financial center and capital city. The Allies dropped close to 2,300 tons of bombs on the city. This bombing mission nearly demolished the Reichsbank, including the presses that printed currency. It was after this that the Reich minister of economics decided to send the gold to a mine at Merkers, 2100 feet beneath the ground and 200 miles southwest of Berlin.

Our 90th Division moved faster than any of the Germans expected, and by the time they tried to retrieve the gold, the paper money, and the art treasures, it was too late. Captured bank officials, trying to escape after the aborted money transfer from the mine, admitted that they were hampered by the partial shutdown of the railway system due to the Easter holidays and by the speed of the American advance.

I made the following diary entries:

April 17, 1945 Heinersgrum, Germany 1200

357th infantry rejoined our Division today, they were finally released from guard duty at the Merkers Mine.

A couple of dough boys passed by our gun company while we were cleaning the gun. "Hey Joe," Verdel called out, "you look like you need a drink." He offered them a bottle of schnapps he had hidden in his pack. "So where did you hide that bag of gold?" Verdel asked the dogfaces. They just laughed him off. "Come on Joe, didn't you bring one for me?" Verdel kept at it.

It is good to have the Combat Team together again.

April 18, 1945 Czech border 1700

The 90th sent a patrol into Czechoslovakia today. We got the word—news blackout is lifted, reporters recorded the event, with photographers. The 90th is the first Division to cross into Czechoslovakia, but our battalion is assigned to patrol the border, on the German side. Auwen says we are heading southeast.

We moved through Germany and stayed close to the Czech border, as ordered. A few fanatical units of the German Army were still fighting, but mostly they were ready to surrender. Das Volk is what the locals called themselves, the German people. Das Volksturm was the rank and file of the Army. The German Army was dissolving into a hodge-podge of Volksturm, Hitler Jugen, highly disorganized veterans, and a few SS. It was crazy; it seemed like the entire German Army was surrendering to us. We didn't have enough POW cages. The surrendering Germans marched away from the front, with one or two American guards or under their own guards. The Germans knew the Russians were coming from the east, and they were in a big hurry to surrender to the Americans. The cruelty of the German Army may only have been matched by the ruthlessness of the Russians. Also, many Russians had lost relatives in Leningrad, which had been firmly under German siege from September 1941 until February 1944, for 900 days. During this time nearly one million Russians perished.

We moved through towns with names impossible to pronounce, like Fletschenreuth, Unterscheida, and Marktleuthen. We'd get into firing position for a day, and then moved on to Wunsiedel, Marktredwitz, and Stieglimuhle. Occasionally, after townspeople displayed the white flag, German soldiers would commence firing. We would burn those towns, hit them with so many artillery shells that they would catch fire.

We started noticing, at this time, that people were buried, or half buried, alongside the road. I saw an emaciated arm sticking up out of a very shallow grave. Why was I seeing so many dead civilians? They appeared much too weak to have been any kind of threat to the German Army, to be part of any organized resistance. We continued to see refugees on the roads, carrying their belongings in baby buggies, carts, knapsacks, little wagons. I was seeing more suffering than I could fathom, and then it got worse.

What we were seeing were the inmates of the Flossenberg Concentration Camp. 15,000 prisoners were evacuated on April 20, in their final death march, just three days before the American Army liberated the camp on April 23rd. When the 90th Division got to Flossenberg, there were only 2000 prisoners alive in the camp. By the time my battalion got there, the Red Cross and Army medical units had moved former inmates to hospitals or clinics. We were taken inside the camp, given a tour of the barracks, shown the crematorium, the mass burial pits. It was horrible.

We were shown movies, right there inside the camp. The Nazis made films as they tortured the prisoners, and the films had been captured. We sat dumbfounded and watched silent films of Nazi officers as they lined up naked women out in the courtyard. An officer would pick one woman and then disappear into their quarters, presumably to rape them. We saw naked women being shoved into ovens, saw their silent screams and their hair catch fire. During the tour of Flossenberg, we saw that one of the Commandants of the camp, Max Koegel, had a lampshade in his office made from human skin. We were told that ashes from the crematorium were shoveled into barrels and sent to the farming districts in Germany to fertilize field crops.

I'd heard about the Natzweiler concentration camp in France, the one the allies discovered in 1944 after the Germans abandoned it. There were survivors of Nazi death camps who had escaped and tried to describe to the civilized world what Hitler's Germany was doing to eliminate the Jews. Nothing compares, however, to seeing it firsthand. After Generals Patton and Eisenhower had toured the Merkers Mine and its treasure, they went to see what was left of Ohrdruf-Nord forced labor camp. Ohrdruf-Nord was a subcamp of Buchenwald, and it was the first concentration camp to be discovered on German soil. The Germans had abandoned it, and most of the prisoners had been taken on a 42-mile final march to Buchenwald. What the Generals saw made them sick. Eisenhower ordered his troops to view the camps. His instructions were to have as many men as possible to see firsthand, the concentration camps, as they were discovered. We knew the Nazis were cruel, but after I visited Flossenberg, I saw evidence of brutality that defies description, and it is incomprehensible how human beings could be so vicious to others. The ruthless disregard for human life, the calculated removal of any shred of human decency, the evidence of barbarism and brutality, what I saw is nearly impossible to describe. The skin and bone bodies of the dead stacked in a shed and sprinkled with lime to reduce the stench, the crematorium ovens, the barracks where 1000 prisoners were kept in wooden bunks that were made for 200, the shallow mass burial pits.

Eisenhower ordered his troops to take a good look, in case we didn't know what we were fighting against.

By May 3rd we were at the Czech border near Rittsteig, Germany, ready to move out with the 357th Infantry when the 11th Panzer Division sent a surrender envoy to the CP at Division HQ. March orders were canceled. We were ordered to cover the road while a convoy of the German 11th Panzer Division surrendered. Hundreds of vehicles and thousands of men passed by in a column, without incident. As the Germans disarmed, one of the officers unbuckled his Luger, and tossed it high in the air, holster and all. It landed with a dull thud right in my lap, as I sat in the back of the truck, with my rifle trained on the surrendering German Army.

Harry Burgam whined, "Dammit, you get all the good stuff, Varano."

Sgt. Auwen said, "What a lucky bastard you are, Johnny."

George Verdel shook his head back and forth and muttered, "Son of a bitch, I don't believe it."

The Luger was the prize handgun confiscated by American GI's during the war. I finally had time to study it and handle it after the surrender parade passed us by, which took all afternoon. The Luger was unique, like something from the future that Buck Rogers would whip out. It was smooth and cold, heavy and black with a long polished muzzle and a magazine that held eight bullets.

I had my Luger for nine years, a war trophy, until after the birth of my first child. My wife was cleaning the dresser drawers and found it hidden under a pile of clothes. She was adamant.

"I will not have a gun in a house with children," my wife said, with no room for argument and I didn't offer any. She had heard enough stories about children accidentally shooting themselves with their father's handgun. I gave the Luger to my brother-in-law, Roy Young, whom we all called Uncle Roy. He had a fine gun collection that he kept at home on his office wall. When he died, his wife, my sister Florence, gave the gun collection to her son by her first marriage, Al Gentile Jr. I've lost contact with Al, but he and my brother Vinny used to be best pals. After Vinny and I visited a war museum in New Orleans, he turned to me and said, "As soon as I feel better, I'm going to go get your gun back." I laughed at his enthusiasm and said sure, not caring either way. As it turned out, my brother did not recover from his illness.

I made the following diary entry:

May 6, 1945 Zwiesel, Germany 0900

We have been moving parallel to the Czech border, but Auwen just announced new orders. We are supposed to march up the main highway into Czechoslovakia through Pilsen and then on to Prague.

Our battalion stopped in Cejkovy, en route to Prague. We were on the way to joining forces with the Russian Army, when we heard the news. It was Monday, the sun shone on our faces in the early afternoon. May 7th, 1945, is a day I will always remember, the day the Germans surrendered and the war in Europe ended. We jumped up and down, hugged each other, sang and danced around. I wrote in my diary:

May 7, 1945 Cejkovy, Czechoslovakia 1500

Our march into Czechoslovakia is joyous, we are liberators again. Everyone lines the streets and roads, cheering as we pass. We moved into Cejkovy, set up what is to be our last combat position because this morning we got a Halt and Cease Fire order and then a few hours ago, we got the message:

"Germany has surrendered unconditionally." Praise be to God. I'll be home soon.

We were the liberators. The Czechs had been oppressed under German occupation for seven years and everyone went nuts with the news. We were the heroes, brave and victorious. The people in the village hung banners, came out in their most festive native dress, dancing in the streets, colors were swirling everywhere, red and white dresses topped with blue and green jumpers and vests, the Czech flag flying. The villagers cooked and served from a cache of food they'd hidden from the Germans. Music played, the schnapps flowed. The town had no electricity, so the Army brought in generators, set poles, strung up wires, provided power so the celebration could continue into the night.

It was after Germany's surrender, in the midst of our victory celebration in Czechoslovakia, that I had this encounter with Ace, Stud's replacement.

It was the early hours of May 9th. Someone shook me violently and said, "Hey Kid, wake up." I grabbed my assailant and tried to wrestle him down. It was an instinctive reaction. I'd been startled out of deep sleep.

"Take it easy, Kid, it's me, Ace."

I was awake now and looked at my watch, 0300. Ace smelled like booze. I looked around. The tent was dimly illuminated by the electric lights strung outside, but it was empty except for me and Ace. The guys were either out celebrating or pulling guard duty. After being sleep deprived for eleven months, I was so tired that all I wanted was my bunk.

And now this. Everyone else called me Varano or Johnny, but not Ace, he had to call me Kid. Although I was one of the youngest GI's in our outfit, I had proved I could handle myself during the war. I wasn't afraid of anything or anybody, including Ace, but maybe I should have been. Ace joined the company at the end of March, as a replacement gunner, after Stud had been wounded and taken out of combat.

"Watch out, he's trouble," one of the non-coms had said. "He used to be a Sergeant, but they took his stripes because he can't stay away from women and booze."

His real name was Norman de Gaulle and he was a Private from Louisiana. "You guys call me Ace," de Gaulle had announced when he was assigned to our gun company. He said this as he sharpened a black-handled six-inch steel chrome switchblade. It was already razor sharp. With a name like de Gaulle, and a slight French accent, the guys had already nicknamed him Frenchie, but no one said it to his face. He always seemed to be sharpening his blade.

Back to my rude awakening in the tent, Ace grabbed me by the shirt and picked me up off the cot so that our faces were within an inch of each other. "Listen Kid, I got to tell you something, I just killed a broad."

The smell of booze on his breath and in his sweat made me nauseous and I was awake now. Ace loved to brag about how many girls he'd fucked the night before, but this was too much. "Why are you telling me this Ace?"

"I got to get it off my chest, I got to confess. You wanted to be a priest, didn't you? You're the only one I can trust. If you tell anyone, I'll kill you, and your family in Connecticut, one by one."

"Ace, I don't want to know, then you don't have to kill me, because I won't be able to tell anyone." I tried to dismiss him, rolled over on my cot, pulled the light wool khaki blanket over my head, even though the night was warm and the wool was itchy. Shut up and leave me alone, Frenchie, I thought.

Everything about Ace was dark, his hair, the pencil thin mustache that made him look like Clark Gable, his aura. He was Mafia, I was sure of it. de Gaulle boasted of the two casinos he owned, one in Louisiana and one in Texas. He was a gambler, a card shark, always looking for a poker hand or a game of craps to bet on. These mobster types seemed to flourish in wartime Europe. Tons of goods were being shipped over from the States, firearms were plentiful, lots of cash to be made on the black market. All the killing going on in the name of war made room for a certain lawlessness. People like de Gaulle had power, connections, it seemed like they could do what they wanted, always knew someone on the inside or up the ranks.

I hoped he would shut up with his macho, sordid story. But he felt the need to unburden himself. He pulled the cover from my head and got in my face. "I picked her out, she was a beauty, great tits," and Ace cupped the imaginary breasts next to his own, his hands bouncing a little with the voluminous weight. I tried to block him out by pulling the pillow over my head. Ace pulled the pillow off, got in my face again and said, "Her name was Heidi, she took a shine to me."

I could not figure out why women were drawn to him.

"She served me food and booze all night," Ace said. "I wanted to choke on those tits, God, she was built, a beauty, long blonde hair, white skin, round face, big eyes, I know a ripe virgin when I see one, I got her off in the woods, and Kid, did I rip her." He grabbed his crotch with one hand, and with a pelvic thrust, he slashed the other arm upward in a tight-fisted uppercut.

"Ace, I'm not interested."

I did not want to be a part of this. I saw where it was going. Hilda, Teresa, Maria, Lisette, Joy, Annette, I'd heard about the string of Ace's exploits, the litany of women's names he'd conquered, details of wild sex, the different positions, how he treated them like meat, how he subdued them and that all women were whores. The village of Cejkovy was too nice a place for a man like him.

"She fought me, so I knocked her out," Ace said, as he demonstrated a quick right hook to the jaw, stopping an inch from my face. He had my attention all right, but I wondered, having sex with an unconscious girl, what is so great about that?

Ace continued to gloat, how he'd had to break the hymen and force his way in, how he'd stripped her naked.

"I've heard enough, Ace."

"But I killed her, I tell you, I killed her." He made a slashing motion across his throat, holding the knife that he'd pulled out of his boot, for the effect. It was as clean as ever and no one ever saw him use it, except for whittling. But now his eyes were bulging, he looked like a crazy man, one who would just as soon kill me as look at me. He was making me sick, but I kept quiet.

"I had to kill her, she'd have fingered me, and it would have been the gallows, or worse." de Gaulle wagged an index finger under my nose. "Don't forget, you talk, you die, and then your mother and father, sister and brother." After this final proclamation, de Gaulle lay down on his cot and was asleep immediately, like a baby.

He's a liar and he's dangerous, I thought, and remembered the fight, the day before, between Ace and Slate. I'd gotten another packet of letters from my sister, Josephine. I was reading them and preparing to respond. Slate was half-lying, half-sitting on his cot next to me, writing a letter to his wife when Ace walked in.

"What the hell are you doing?" Ace asked, looking for trouble.

"What's it to you?" Slate answered, not looking up.

Ace walked over and peered over Slate's shoulder. "You think she's true to you while we're over here? She's probably screwing the mailman."

Slate rose from his cot, hot with anger but cold and deliberate. "Come on outside, I'm going to beat your ass."

Slate was a big man, strong, a farmer from South Dakota. He outmatched Ace, but Ace fought dirty.

They started beating on each other, two animals ready to kill, but we pulled them apart. This kind of violence was just below the surface. I wondered if we'd all been reduced to subhuman after eleven months of killing, and if it was too late for any of us to go home, even though the war in Europe was over.

I wished I hadn't helped to pull them apart, I wished Slate had finished Ace off that morning, or at least put him in the hospital. Slate had been with "C" Battery since early in the war, he was a good guy and we'd fought together throughout Europe.

The next morning, at roll call, I stood at attention. We were about to get our daily assignments when Captain Bremer marched up to the podium, escorted on each side by MP's. He was having difficulty addressing the company. His voice was breaking up, and I thought maybe there was a loose wire in the PA system, but Bremer didn't look right.

"I cannot believe that one of my men would be involved," Bremer paused, "involved in such a hideous act of butchering," another pause, "butchering an innocent girl."

Bremer was usually stoic, but this morning he fought to control his emotions, his anger. "Anyone with information, report to me immediately or you'll become an accessory to the crime. As for the murderer, he'll wish he was never born."

At this point, Captain Bremer turned away. He looked angry enough to spit. One of the MP's spoke to him. Bremer stepped off the podium and pointed to the bulletin board that held the day's assignments. There was a poster with a picture of a smiling young girl with a round face framed by long blonde braids, pinned on top of her head.

Chapter Eight

Occupation, VJ Day, Back Home

I had never once thought of killing a fellow GI, until I realized how easy it would be to get rid of Private de Gaulle. I could not get him out of my head. Ace was a Mafioso dirt bag and he boasted of committing murder, while threatening to have my family killed back in Connecticut. He treated everyone like scum and I would be doing the Army a favor if I made him disappear. I was very troubled with these thoughts, as I walked across the compound in search of Father Bastian, the company Chaplain.

I took a deep breath. It was the middle of spring, May, 1945. I smelled lily, jasmine, and wild rose on the breeze, and the festive feeling of this farming village of Cejkovy, Czechoslovakia was accented by buzzing bees and flitting butterflies. At any other time, it would have pleased me. With Germany's unconditional surrender, the War in Europe was technically over, but Allied troops were still heavily armed. We had guns, alcohol, and plenty of time on our hands, while we waited to be reassigned as the Occupational Force.

I pulled up short when I found the Chaplain's quarters and rapped on the wooden frame that held up the entrance to his tent. He was a Captain.

"May I have a moment with you, sir?" I said.

"Come in soldier," Father Bastian said. He extended his hand to me and instead of saluting, I clasped his hand. I knew the Chaplain from having attended Mass, but he did not know me.

"Father, I am Private First Class John Varano with Charlie Battery, 343rd Field Artillery Battalion. I wish to speak to you about a private matter."

The Chaplain offered me a folding chair but I was too nervous to sit. He wore a Roman collar because, like me, he was Catholic. We both wore green combat fatigues and dark leather boots. The priest was a few inches taller than me. Father Bastian cleared some space on his desk, moved his helmet which, unlike mine, had a white cross stenciled on the front.

"How can I help you, John," the Chaplain asked kindly. He must have seen my anxiety.

"I am a Catholic, Father, and I need to give you my Confession," I said.

The priest removed a purple stole from his desk drawer, kissed it and draped it over his shoulders. Now he understood how serious this was to me. He crossed himself. The quality of light seemed to change in the Chaplain's tent, as we moved from the secular to the sacramental realm. I sat down on the folding chair and intoned the words of my youth, "Bless me father for I have sinned, my last General Absolution was four weeks ago."

I thought I could smell incense and see the flicker of candlelight and, out of the corner of my eye, the color of stained glass window saints. The priest carefully tented his fingers and I began my story.

"Five days ago," I said, "a soldier who calls himself 'Ace' yanked me out of my cot, I mean deep sleep. He'd been out most of the night, drinking and carousing. This wasn't the first time he'd done this to me but this was the worst. I told him to go away but he grabbed me and shoved his face into mine, his breath stinking of booze." I proceeded to recount to the priest the grisly story, in detail, that Ace had forced upon me in the middle of the night.

"The next morning, that was last Saturday," I explained, "Captain Bremer, at roll call, ordered anyone with information concerning the death of a sixteen year old local girl to come forward. Since then, the MP's have been circulating flyers with a picture of a girl with pale braids tied on top of her head. She was real pretty and her name was Heidi."

There were a few moments of silence. Then the priest asked, "Was there anyone else in the tent to hear Ace's story?"

"No," I answered.

"Do you have any physical evidence linking Ace to the crime?" Father Bastian asked.

"No."

"Any eye witnesses?"

"Not to my knowledge."

"Do you think Ace was drunk?"

"He stunk of alcohol and he passed out right after he finished his story."

"It would be your word against his if you reported Ace to the Captain."

"Yes, my word against his, Father, but Captain Bremer has been transferred, and I don't know to whom I would be reporting."

Father Bastian and I continued to talk.

The priest prayed with me. He convinced me to wait, to talk to him before I made any rash decisions. I walked back to my tent and felt less guilty, less desperate, and no longer like committing murder.

Before the week was over, Ace had been transferred out of Czechoslovakia, good riddance, no one asked how, where, or why. My moral dilemma was put on the back burner. Ace was gone, but it bothers me to this day, and I wonder if I did the right thing by keeping silent. I also wonder why only Ace disappeared so quickly when the rest of us were wrapped up in red tape, the layers of Army paperwork in duplicate and triplicate.

Now the questions were, when am I going home, when am I getting transferred out? But this vital information was held back until I was reassigned in Weiden, Germany. I made an entry in my diary:

May 30, 1945 0800 Cejkovy

> New orders came down from HQ today, we are leaving Czechoslovakia and going to our new base in Germany as Occupational Forces. My gun crew, Charlie Company, has been disbanded, only Corporal George Verdel is still with me, by some kind of luck or mistake or problem of logistics, as the Army likes to say, but he is more than ready to be discharged. Sgt. Auwen is gone, who knows where, Willy Tushar, my best friend, is gone, as is George P. Young and Jose 'Hey Amigo' Alcorta. We were so close, like a family, and now I feel kind of empty, demoralized.

The 90th Division arrived in Germany, truckloads of soldiers and officers and convoys of equipment, but we were no longer the 90th Infantry Division, we were now the Third Army's Occupational Force. We took over three city blocks in the town of Weiden, in the district Oberphalz, in the region of Bavaria. Bavaria is in southeastern Germany and shares borders with Austria and Czechoslovakia, now the Czech Republic. Private Eddie Russo, an Italian from Ohio, became my new bunk mate. We stowed our gear and were called out to stand at attention by the new CO.

"Men, listen up. You may be wondering why you are still here, when your buddies have shipped out. Well, believe me, no one has shipped out. They are waiting in line somewhere else. We have a job to do. If you have earned 85 points, you can get in line to go home. But if you have earned less than 85 points, you are part of the Third Army's Occupational Force. You will occupy the German State of Bavaria and will be trained to fight in Japan. Full dress inspection at 1200 hours. General Patton arrives tomorrow to inspect his troops, company dismissed."

I had 70 points. The next morning was Saturday. I stood at attention, out in the hot sun, in my dress uniform, khaki shirt and tie, Eisenhower jacket, pants, and polished boots. A plastic helmet had replaced our metal helmet, since no bombs were dropping, and the helmet was sprayed with a green enamel paint that shined. I was polished, pressed, buttoned, cleaned and pinned until I had passed two dress inspections. What a sight to see, General George S. Patton, in the flesh. Patton's aid drove him by in his jeep, while Patton stood ramrod straight, ringed fingers resting easily on the windshield. Patton's two ivory handled pistols flashed white in their holster, one at each hip. He had four stars sparkling on his helmet, belt buckle, epaulets. Patton stood so tall and still, we got a good look at the medals and ribbons, stripes pinned and sewn onto his lapels, jacket sleeves, and above his breast pocket. His face looked like it had been sculptured from granite and his eyes seemed to bore a hole in anything or anyone they focused on. The General's jeep halted in front of the platform that had been erected for the occasion, and he climbed up the stairs. He spoke into the microphone mounted on a podium.

"I want to thank the men of the 90th Infantry Division for being the best goddamned Division that a General could hope to lead. It has been an honor to lead you in victory over the Germans in Europe."

Cheers broke out among the troops, even though we were supposed to be at attention.

"You may have heard that I have been assigned duties as Military Governor of Bavaria."

More cheers. "I hope to be seeing more of you men. Carry on and when your grandson asks you, what did you do in the war Grandpa, tell him you fought the good fight with the great Third Army, you beat the goddamned Germans, and you made General Patton proud."

We cheered for five minutes and no one tried to stop us. Patton was our man, our leader. He was profane and controversial, outspoken and cunning. The war for us had turned around and gained momentum in the Allies' favor once Patton had been given command. He was not a good politician, like General Eisenhower, but Patton was a great warrior. I did not know how long he would last as Military Governor of Bavaria, but I sincerely hoped I would see him again. He was the only General I wanted to serve under.

Our company was dismissed and I returned to my barracks. I got my Diary out of the duffel bag to write about Patton's speech when Eddie, my bunkmate, strolled in.

"Hey Varano, Corporal Verdel is looking for you," Eddie said.

I hopped off my bunk and asked, "Which way did he go?"

"He's in the canteen. He says it's important."

I wanted to talk to George Verdel, I wanted to ask him what he thought of Patton's speech. He was the only guy left of my old company. I walked across the barracks, which was like walking down the block, since we had taken over a neighborhood in the town of Weiden. I walked past the non-commissioned officer's quarters to the little storefront cafe that had been converted into an Army canteen. I saw Verdel sitting at a table by himself, reading *Stars and Stripes*, the Army's Weekly Newspaper.

"Hey Verdel, I heard you were looking for me."

"Yeah, Varano, I got a favor to ask you."

I sat down next to him. Verdel was a man of few words, but while I waited for him to gather his thoughts, I couldn't help but ask, "What did you think of Patton's speech?"

"Johnny, same old shit, different town."

"Well, George, if I have to be in the Army, I want Patton to be my General." Verdel looked up. His cold, pale blue eyes peered at me above his glasses, which had slipped down, as usual.

"Johnny, that is what I need to talk to you about, goddamn it," Verdel grumbled. He pushed his glasses back up on his nose. I saw some kind of emotion in his eyes, maybe regret. I was not used to seeing any emotion in Verdel. He was seven years older than me and somewhat embittered by life, but we were friends, and we'd fought side by side for the last year, the most exciting year of our lives, although Verdel would never admit it.

"What is it George," I asked, since Verdel seemed unsure how to continue.

"I got my discharge orders today. I am moving out tomorrow at 0900."

"Congratulations, George, I am going miss you. You are a lucky son of a gun." We both stood up and hugged. Verdel was feeling something and I was fighting back tears, both glad for him and sad for me. I would be totally abandoned then by my gun company, the thing that made the War not just bearable but meaningful and sometimes even funny—being with a group of guys that went to hell and back together.

"Listen Johnny, I need you to do something for me."

"Anything, George," and I meant it.

Verdel pulled an envelope out of his jacket breast pocket. It was tattered, but used to be ivory colored when it was new, a long business sized envelope, addressed to:

Mrs. Agnes Verdel
125 Main Street
Deer Park, Washington State
United States of America

Verdell opened the unsealed envelope and pulled out one-hundred-dollar bills, he counted fifty of them, face up, showing Ben Franklin. He slid the bills back into the envelope and said, "Please mail this money to my mother in the States. I know you are going home as soon as you can."

"George, why are you giving this to me?" I didn't say I did not want the responsibility, or that it would be better for him to mail it since he was being discharged and I wasn't. I didn't ask him where he got all this money, because the only thing that really mattered to me was why me and why now?

"Johnny, you are the only person I trust."

"But George, you'll be back home, probably in a month or two, and who knows where I'll end up. What if I die in Japan?"

"Naw kid, with everyone praying for you, and the way you love your family, you'll be home before me, because I'm not going home, ever, I am done with that. I'll probably get rolled by some prostitute in New York City and end up drunk in the gutter, but hey kid, I am going to have a hell of a time." George punched me in the arm. We did a fierce bear hug, and then stepped apart.

"Okay, George, I'll take care of it for you."

Verdel grabbed my hand and shook it. "I trust you Johnny, don't worry. I saved a few bucks for myself."

I was even more reluctant now to say goodbye to Verdel. I put the envelope carefully in my jacket pocket and buttoned the flap. "Goodbye, George," I said, "God be with you."

"Have a good life, Johnny."

I felt like we'd never see each other again, and I was right.

I went back to my bunk, put on my money belt and stuffed the thick envelope into one of the compartments. I am going to have to sleep with this, I thought. Where did Verdel get the money? I'd been with him most days and most nights since we'd started fighting the Germans after D-Day, and now I realized I didn't know him. If he'd saved every penny that the Army paid him for the last two years, then he'd have maybe $2000.00. So where did he get the rest? Did he steal Deutschmarks from dead Germans and pay someone to exchange them? Did he find a sack of money on the road that fell off a German truck? Verdel was a man of few words, but I did know that he loved his mother, hated his father, and trusted me more than he trusted himself. I hoped I would be back in the States soon and I'd mail the money right off, special delivery, signature required. This set me thinking of my sister and mother, and I pulled the latest letter from home out of the plywood locker that I kept next to my bunk. It was an army green footlocker and I kept all my personal effects in it. I kept the key to the lock in my wallet. I reread the letter.

My Dearest Johnny!
New Britain, Connecticut May 8, 1945

The War is over! Germany surrendered! You have no idea what is happening here in the Hardware City of the World, where we have more factories than anywhere. You know the population of your hometown has swelled from 60,000 to 90,000 people, and everyone is celebrating, factory whistles blowing, people running out in the streets, car horns honking, the buses are delayed and no one can get on, they are full. John you can't believe how these people are jumping out of their skins, laughing, hugging, crying.

Including Mrs. Antonucci from next door, even though she lost her son Jim (he was my boyfriend at one time, so was Gary, and he died overseas too—very bad luck to be my boyfriend). Anyway, Mrs. Antonucci comes out and tells our mother, "Gracia, I am so glad that your son Johnny made it and my Jimmy died for freedom."

Mama hugs Mrs. Antonucci and says, "Sara, Jimmy is with God, waiting for you up in heaven."

Everyone is kissing, even strangers and you know what, there's a band out in the street right now, Mr. Chiotio with his accordion, and there is a bugle, a trumpet, two clarinets and a saxophone. No one is going to work. The women are out in their housedresses, dancing the jig.

The shop whistles have not stopped. And you won't believe what Mama and her girlfriends did. They were out celebrating on the corner of Webster and Arch Street. They flagged down the bus and ended up in Hartford.

When Mama got home she said," I didn't even know where I was going, but we heard there were parades."

I don't know how Mama and her comares got back from Hartford, but they did.

High School bands are out on Main Street, spontaneous parades, people are coming out of nowhere, there is no room to even move, cars are stopped on the street. You can walk a lot faster than you can drive anywhere.

The churches are swelled with people. Mama could have burnt the church down with the number of candles she lit for you, on VE Day and every day before.

Papa is also out dancing in the streets, toasting with his homemade wine, and the police are out there too. I mean someone could have robbed a bank today and no one would have cared, that is why they closed the banks and the stores, the schools, everything, the offices, factories, no one can be contained. All businesses had to close. We are so happy, we can't wait to see you.

All My Love,
Josephine

I decided to write a letter home:

Dear Josephine,
June 15, 1945 Weiden, Germany

    I just reread your letter from May 8th and I can see Mama dancing around with her comares. General Patton spoke to us today, he is the best leader we have ever had. It was his farewell speech to the 90th Division and I got a little choked up.
    Corporal George Verdel said goodbye to me today, he is sure that I will get home before he does, because Mama goes to church everyday to pray for me. Verdel has a lot of seniority over me, so he is in line for a discharge, and now it is just the paperwork. I have a new bunkmate, Eddie Russo. He's an Italian from Ohio. We hit it off right away, but I miss the guys from Charlie Company, more than I can say.

I quickly signed the letter, Love, Johnny, before I started saying something like I wasn't really coming home because I wasn't eligible for discharge and would probably die in Japan. I mean one can dodge the bullet for just so long, and I didn't want my mother and sisters, father and brother to think that all their prayers were in vain.

We did our time as the Occupational Force. It was both better and worse than fighting. One hot day, late in June, I returned to the barracks with a book tucked under my arm from the library. I still have it, in fact, 60 years later. It sits on my bookshelf at home, Hoyt's New Encyclopedia of Practical Quotations compiled by Kate Louise Roberts, copyright 1940, provided by The American Red Cross, Weiden Branch. When I was a block from my building, I turned the corner and saw a row of soldiers lining the sidewalk. The queue wrapped around the courtyard and wound into the house. I pushed my way in, past the GI's. I walked up to the second floor where my bunk was and saw the line as it continued up to the third floor. Then I heard screaming from the fourth floor attic. It was the screams of a woman.

I started to push my way up towards the attic and one of the GI's said, "Hey, get in line asshole, like the rest of us."

"What's going on?" It was bad, whatever it was.

"What do you think, dumb fuck, the maid is giving it away for free today."

I thought I'd recognized the screams. It was Anna, the young German girl who came in a couple of times a week to cook and clean and do our laundry. I pushed my way up to the third floor and saw guys with their pants down, anxious to get into the attic. Most of them already had a hard-on. The guys were starved for sex. Anna's screams got louder and I said, "Hey, leave her alone."

One of the GI's said, "Hey, mother fucker, who asked you? Get the hell out of here."

Before I could answer, a couple of MP's shouldered their way up the stairs and started arresting GI's who now could not get their pants up fast enough. Someone had called the Military Police, and in about five minutes, everyone scattered or was hauled away in paddy wagons. Anna was still screaming. The MP's took her to the hospital.

I moved quickly into my room, stuffed the book in my footlocker and exited the building. Everything was going to hell. I caught up with Eddie, who had the same idea, get out fast.

"Varano, I told you the 'No Fraternization' rule was full of shit. Look what the Army has to deal with now. If news of the gang bang gets out, the Army will crucify us. I just volunteered for an extra shift of patrol duty."

"I'm right behind you, Eddie."

Eddie and I did a six hour shift on patrol instead of the usual three, and Eddie talked to me almost non-stop about the German girl that he'd just met. He wanted so much to impress her but did not know where to begin.

"Come with me, Varano, put in a good word for me."

I turned him down. Eddie badgered me. Finally, one evening, I jumped the fence with Eddie, and then got arrested for being out of uniform. My breast pocket was unbuttoned. I also had an illegible pass. Eddie's forgery department let me down.

I was put on latrine duty for a month, and the Captain of the Military Police gave me a serious warning, one more infraction and I'd be sent to the Pacific.

The next time Eddie asked me to go with him to see his future German girlfriend, I said, "What are we waiting for?"

We bribed the guards on duty, Private Johnson and Private O'Malley. I promised to look the other way tomorrow night when Johnson and O'Malley jumped the fence and Eddie slipped them each a ten dollar bill. We left the barracks right after dark. We avoided the MP's patrol route by going through backyards. Eddie and I jumped over fences for about a mile, weaving our way through the sleepy city of Weiden.

"Here we are," Eddie said. We stood outside the back entrance of a sturdy, three story, red brick house. "Millie's parents own this place. They are the landlords," Eddie told me. Eddie knocked on the back door, a couple of quick raps, and a short, elderly man answered.

"Guten Abend," Eddie said.

"Guten Abend," the man said. He recognized Eddie and invited us into the back hall that led to his family kitchen.

"I brought my bunkmate, Private John Varano, to meet you," Eddie said, suddenly a little shy.

Millie and her mother got up from the kitchen table.

"Millie, this is John, my roommate," Eddie said, and then "John, I would like you to meet Millie."

Millie and I shook hands and I felt an electric shock pass between us.

"It's my pleasure," I said.

Millie lowered her eyes and blushed. Maybe she felt something too. She wore a blue and white checkered dress, fitted at the waist, with a full skirt that fell below her knees. Her eyes were clear blue and she had blonde hair that curled softly to her shoulders. Her pale skin made me think of warm porcelain.

Eddie brought gifts of canned meat and soap that he'd requisitioned from the Supply Sergeant, and I'd brought chocolate bars and American cigarettes. Soon, Eddie and I were drinking coffee and eating strudel with Hans and Anna Fick and their daughter Millie. I learned that her full name was Melanie.

Eddie had carefully explained to me, before our little excursion, that my job was to build him up, to make him look good, to vouch for him, give examples of what a wonderful guy he was, so that Millie might fall for Eddie as hard as Eddie had fallen for her.

Millie was distracting me from my mission. She was beautiful, shy, and nineteen years old. After an hour in her company, I was smitten. I understood why Eddie wanted to make it with her because she was not only beautiful, but refined, compassionate, and came from a good family. She spoke English better than I did. By the time she sat down to play piano, after we'd eaten, I was completely under her spell. She was more beautiful than Lana Turner, who was fresh in my mind. We'd seen Turner's new film, "Slightly Dangerous," in the Recreation Hall two nights earlier.

We returned to our room in the house that was our barracks, and I told Eddie I was not cut out for match making and he would do fine without me. I'd already told Millie everything I knew about Eddie, everything that was worth telling, and I hardly knew him anyway.

A few weeks later, Eddie started talking to me about Gretta, this beautiful German girl he was in love with and I said, "What happened to Millie?"

Eddie said, "Oh, she was too stuck up and formal for me, John. I mean how much coffeecake can one man eat? And I am not one to sit in the parlor and listen to the piano."

I wanted to tell Eddie he was a blind fool to let go of Millie, but instead I said, "Do you mind if I go see her then?"

"No problem, Johnny, if she's your type, go for it, but if you ask me, she's kind of a cold fish. German girls are either loose or tight, there is no in between, not like the French women. French girls are moody, but they know how to make a man feel like a man."

That night I wrote in my diary:

Weiden, Germany, 1500 July 1st, 1945

> Eddie told me he is done with Millie and I am trying to get up the nerve to go see her on my own. I know this sounds crazy, but I think I am in love with her.
>
> I am afraid to go see her. I am sure she will reject me. She is so beautiful and educated and refined, and I am part of the conquering Army. I have to disobey orders to even go to her house. She probably thinks I'm crude and stupid, but I can't stop thinking of her. I have to see Millie again.

That night I stuffed my pockets with gifts, paid off the guards with money and promises, and jumped the fence. I knocked at the Fick's back door and Millie answered. Her blue eyes registered surprise, and I thought maybe she was glad to see me, the way she welcomed me in. Her blonde hair was pinned up in a bun, instead of touching her shoulders, and I noticed the curve of her long neck, and how some wispy curls had come loose and were reaching down to the collar of her light blue sweater. Millie was a sweater girl all right.

I unloaded my pockets on the kitchen table, soap and candy, cigarettes and small cans from my Army rations. Millie's father joined us for coffee, and he was so pleased to get American cigarettes. He shook my hand vigorously and slapped me on the back. Anna, Millie's mother, seemed glad to see me also.

"Hans Jr., my older brother, got Papa hooked on American cigarettes," Millie told me, as we moved into the living room. "He is doing a shift at the hospital tonight. I'd like you to meet him."

"Is he a doctor?" I asked. I was uneasy about meeting Hans, but not yet sure why.

"Yes, he was drafted as an Army surgeon with a German Tank Division, but our prayers were answered when he was discharged six months ago."

Now I was getting a bad feeling. "Discharged?" I asked.

"Yes, John, he was hit by enemy fire, but he's recovered and Hans is working again at Weiden Hospital, since May."

I did not want to talk about Hans.

"I brought something for you, Millie," I said, and unfolded the sheet music that I'd tucked into my shirt behind my back. I'd lifted it from the Army Recreation Hall. It was the top forty tune, "The White Cliffs of Dover." Millie smoothed out the pages and set them up on the piano. Her long delicate fingers glided over the keys. Together we sang:

> There'll be bluebirds over, The white cliffs of Dover, Tomorrow,
> just you wait and There'll be love and laughter, And peace ever after,
> Tomorrow when the world is free.

I looked up at the old grandfather clock that graced her living room. It was after 9 o'clock.

"I have to go back to the barracks," I said. "I had a real good time, Millie. Can I come see you again tomorrow?"

"Yes, I would like that very much, Johnny."

Hans was waiting to meet me when I arrived at Millie's house the next evening. Hans was ten years older than Millie and seven years older than me. He was a skilled doctor who almost died of injuries received while serving as a medic for a German Tank Division. We swapped combat stories. He was proud of his battle wounds and pulled up his shirt to show me the incision across his back that went from shoulder to waist, as if someone had tried to cut him in half. With Millie as translator, Hans told me how fierce the fighting was at St. Lo.

"Yes," I said, "I remember St. Lo, I thought we'd never break through."

Hans told me that he was wounded just outside of Metz and I said yes, I thought we'd never get out of the mud in Metz.

Hans asked, "Which Division were you in, John?"

I said, "the 90th Division."

"Was is das?"

I repeated, "the 90th Division."

"Verdammt! You were like a plague on us, we could not shake you."

"What Division were you in Hans?"

"The 3rd Panzer Division."

I thought, holy crap, the 3rd Panzer Division, it could have been my Howitzer that ripped a hole in him. It was too late to undo the damage that our two armies had done, and it was too late to stop my feelings for Millie. Sometimes I almost wished I'd had more self-control and had not jumped the fence with Eddie. Things got tangled up badly after I fell in love with Millie. I became a regular at Stockerhutweg #8. That was Millie's address. I was there most evenings. One afternoon in late July, I got off guard duty early. We'd been seeing each other for a month, but it seemed like a lot longer. I hustled back to the barracks, shaved, put on Millie's favorite cologne, Midnight Blue I think it was called, and bought a box of candy at a shop on the way to Stockerhutweg #8. I was free until midnight. The Army was letting up on the non-fraternization policy. There was no way Uncle Sam could keep an Occupational Force of lonely young men from seeing the lovely local women.

I knocked and Millie opened the door. Something was wrong. She turned away from me instead of moving towards me with that light in her eyes, the light that I lived for. Usually, I stepped into the foyer and she'd put her arms around my neck and give me a light kiss. But this time she turned away, walked back into her kitchen. From the right side of her face, I could see that she'd been crying. She was trying to hide from me.

"Millie, what is it?"

She turned towards me for a split second and I saw that the left side of her face was red and swollen.

"What happened?" I said.

"I walked into a door," Millie said.

"What happened?" I asked again

"Fritz hit me."

"Where is he?"

"Please, Johnny, you will only make it worse. He told me not to associate with the American soldier or I would pay the price."

Fritz and his wife lived on the third floor of Millie's building. Millie's family rented to them. I'd checked out everyone on Millie's block, using what connections I had in the world of Army Intelligence. He was a Nazi warden before the German surrendered. He was the one who collected fees and spied on everyone in the neighborhood, he ratted them out to the SS or to the Gestapo if it served his purposes. He was a thief, a coward, a bully, and a Nazi sympathizer. I was going to save the Army time and money in prosecution fees and kill him on the spot.

I shook free of Millie's restraining arm and took the back stairs two at a time up to the third floor. No one was home. I returned to Millie's apartment. I would wait.

"Please don't do anything, Johnny, he'll kill you. I'll be okay, it was only a slap. If anything happens to you, I don't know what I'll do."

"Don't worry, Millie, I won't do anything stupid, I just want to have a man to man talk with him. No one is going to knock you around."

Millie's mother Anna appeared and stood beside her daughter. She approved of my position, as Millie translated it, and the two women retreated inside their apartment.

I waited for Fritz to come home. There was only one entrance to the building and it was around back. There were three stairs that led to the door, which was always unlocked, and today, because of nice weather, the door stood open. I took my carbine out of the shoulder strap, sat down on the top step and laid the rifle across my lap, so that it barred the doorway. I removed the gun clip and put it in the pocket of my Eisenhower jacket. I did not want to kill Fritz. I only wanted to convince him to leave Millie alone.

No more than fifteen minutes went by and Fritz appeared with his wife trailing behind him. I stood up and Fritz ran into my gun.

"Halt," I said.

His wife started screaming. Fritz yelled at her, "Mach Schell! Ruf die Polizei!"

She ran. I did not need anyone to translate, "Hurry, call the MP's."

I set my gun down and grabbed Fritz by the shirt. I gave him a head butt in the face and he crashed into the wall. Fritz bounced off the wall and grabbed me in a bear hug. I landed a volley of punches to his kidneys and ribs. Soon we were down on the floor. He was bigger, meaner, more experienced than I was, but I was fueled by righteous rage. Somehow I got on top of Fritz and got my hands around his throat. A white heat blazed before my eyes. I squeezed his windpipe and he gasped, unable to scream, his mouth open. I pressed harder. Hate was the only thing I felt. I tightened my grip on the big man's throat.

I felt hands on my wrists, hands on my waist, and then heard voices, "Hey, take it easy soldier," and "you don't want to kill a civilian." It took two big MP's to pull me off.

Fritz got to his feet. His wife ran to him. Millie and her mother came out of their apartment. The women were bordering on hysteria. I was still trying to get at Fritz, who was choking and gasping and holding his throat. The MP's dragged me by the legs and stuffed me into the jeep. "You are under arrest soldier."

I came to my senses. "What! You're taking his word over mine? He's a Nazi. Go check his apartment, third floor." I did not want to go to the MP's headquarters to see the Captain again, the one who promised to send me to Japan for a friggin uniform violation.

More MP's showed up, and while two of them contained me and Fritz, the other two searched the third floor apartment. After about 30 minutes, a nice cooling off period, the MP's returned, carrying a box of papers and files and a ledger. They let me go and carried Fritz off, in handcuffs. I straightened my uniform, tucked in my shirt and put the gun clip back in my rifle. Millie cleaned me up and bandaged my cuts. I would hurt a lot more the next day, but I was still running on adrenaline and surprised by the depth of my feelings for Millie and the blindness of my rage against someone who had hurt her. I told Millie to take care of herself and that I'd be back tomorrow. I needed to lay low for awhile.

I managed to stay out of jail after the run in with Fritz and the MP's, but it did not deter me. Whenever I wasn't on duty, I was with Millie. I was like a member of the family. We went to mass together on Sunday mornings at the Church of Saint Peter, das Kirche aus Heiliger Peter. It was a Sunday in the beginning of August, and after mass, Millie invited me to join her family for a stroll in the park, a German tradition, einen Spaziergang durch den Park. The weather was perfect, the trees were leafed out, and the park was lush, partly due to recent rain. The Germans knew how to make things beautiful. Multicolored pansies bloomed in circles underneath the chestnut trees. There was a pond in the center of the park, and geese flew down to swim and rest and feed.

Millie and I held hands. We laughed and talked. Her parents walked behind us. We took a circuitous route home because Hans and Anna were collecting wild mushrooms to make a dish for Sunday dinner. Their basket was nearly full of morels.

Then Millie grabbed my arm and pulled me up short. She pointed ahead at five young men who had materialized from behind a stand of Poplar trees. They looked like Hitler Jugen, although they were out of uniform. They wore black leather jackets, their heads were shaved. I could see pipes and chains poking out from under their jackets. They looked hungry, their faces chiseled with hate. One of the group started yelling, Schweinehund! Pig Dog! Vernichtung zum Amerikaner! Death to the American. I turned to Millie and her parents.

"Run!" I said. "Now!" And the three of them took off.

I pulled out the P38 from my shoulder holster, took aim with both hands, and squeezed off a couple rounds a few inches above the heads of the vigilantes. The young German hoodlums scattered, and then I knew they did not have guns, only pipes and chains with which to beat their victims.

When I got back to the barracks Sunday night, after assuring Millie and her parents that they were out of danger, I wondered if I was being stupid, putting everyone at risk. I was in love, but in post-war Germany, I had to keep my head. The vigilantes that I encountered were known as Werewolves, and we had plenty of reports of their guerrilla warfare against, not only American soldiers, but other Germans who were considered anti-Nazi or pro-American. Millie wasn't really safe, and even when I thought I should stay away from the Fritz family, I knew I could not. However, we did not stray far from Millie's neighborhood after that, which was less than five city blocks from my barracks, a zone well protected by the Allies. There were no more leisurely walks in the park. I tried to take a buddy or two and their dates along, if we were going to the movies. If we went out to eat, I would invite Millie's brother Hans and his wife. Strength in numbers was not only a tactic used by pro-Nazi Werewolf gang members.

As part of our infantry training for the Pacific, we watched films on the Battle of Iwo Jima that took place back in February and newsreels about the Battle of Okinawa which was finally captured only the month before in July.

We went out for field exercises in the undeveloped plots of land outside Weiden. My company practiced with bayonets. Dummies were lined up and we had to pierce them and pull the bayonet out, thrust, pull back, and I thought to myself, this is just like friggin' basic training all over again. Have I been demoted to a grunt, a dogface to be trampled in the jungles of the Pacific or eaten up by jungle rot or malaria? I think the Army was insulting us with these maneuvers to keep us fighting mad. No one wanted to think about what our chance of success would be with an amphibious land invasion of the home Islands of Japan.

The next day we were in foxholes learning how to lob hand grenades and how to react defensively. Throw and duck, how much training does it take? We pitched dummy grenades, ones without explosives inside. A soldier, two foxholes down, side-armed a grenade instead of lobbing it, and the grenade slammed into my hand, solid metal, like being hit by a spiky cast iron ball. My hand bled and began to swell. A trip to the infirmary earned me a sling. My hand was painted red with mercurochrome, wrapped in gauze, and I was told to rest.

After two days of ice packs and a lot of sympathy from Millie, I was back in the field. This time I carried a full pack, thirty-five pounds, and marched mile after mile, in the hot sun. I thought, what is this, am I back in Barry, Wales? This stinks, where was George Verdel when I needed him? No one swore as good as he did. I could hear him beside me grumbling, muttering, and complaining, something like, this: *cock suckers, this mother fucking Army, sons of bitches, I'm not going to Japan, goddamn it.* But Verdel was gone, and I marched on, silently. No one, but no one, wanted to fight the kamikaze Japanese, an Army that was trained to strap bombs to their backs and dive under American tanks, an Air Force that flew one way missions in planes full of explosives to dive bomb American war ships, a society of people who believed that it was honorable to kill yourself and your family rather than face the unbearable shame of surrender.

I wrote in my diary:

August 13, 1945 1300 Weiden, Germany

We got orders today, Sergeant Miller announced we are going on maneuvers for two weeks, starting tomorrow, pack your gear, get a good night's sleep. Scuttlebutt has spread through the barracks

like wildfire, we are not coming back from maneuvers. We will
be put on trucks to ports of embarkation and then shipped out to
Japan.

Morale can't be any lower.

I packed my equipment and went to see Millie. I told her I was leaving
for two weeks in the field, and there were rumors we were not coming back
to Weiden but going straight to Japan after intensive field training. Millie
started to cry. "Nothing has changed between us," I said. "I still want to
marry you." "I will wait for you Johnny, until the end of time," Millie said. I
stayed at Millie's house until 0300.

Later that day, we were on the march, and the farther we got from Weiden,
the worse I felt. I might not see Millie again. God knows if my luck will hold
out. It was like starting another war in another part of the world, thousands
of miles away from people that I loved. Things looked bleak even though the
day was bright.

It was warm, clear skies, a summer day in Europe. At 1400, a dispatch
courier on a motorcycle caught up with our column and spoke to Captain
Franklin who was leading the march. Franklin signaled for the column to
halt. I saw him talk to the courier and a smile spread across his face. The
Captain turned to us and said, "I have good news for you gentlemen, Japan
has surrendered, unconditionally. The war is over."

An electric shock passed through the column. One minute we were on
the road to maneuvers, the next minute we were going wild. I hooted and
hollered, jumped up and down, and hugged Eddie. My gun was loaded and
I had plenty of live ammunition, but I knew better than to start shooting.
Bottles of whisky appeared from nowhere and were quickly consumed. The
bottles were passed around: French cognac and liqueur, German beer, wine,
schnapps, and Russian vodka. Soon there were a bunch of drunken soldiers
shooting off round after round of live ammo from rifles, carbines, and pistols.
The MP's just threw up their hands. VJ Day could not be contained. I knew
I needed to keep my wits about me. I did not drink because I had plenty of
opportunity to see the disastrous combination of booze and live ammunition.

We reached Weiden sometime in the evening, and our barracks and the
entire camp were in an uproar. All discipline gone, it was like a monster
unleashed, and until the alcohol was consumed and sweated out with dancing
and hugging, singing and shouting, until the rounds of fire were depleted and
the soldiers collapsed into beds, on the sidewalk, or out in the fields, the
monster would not be contained. The next morning, the casualty count began,
some missing fingers, some serious wounds, some deaths.

I went to Millie's house as soon as I could get away. I was surprised to
see German civilians celebrating. Hitler was never popular in Bavaria and

the war's end was reason to celebrate. Millie's house was filled with family, friends, and neighbors. I got a handshake from her brother Hans and back slapping from her father Hans, hugs from her mother and sister-in-law. I got kisses from her neighbors and girlfriends. Millie was being the gracious hostess, and I could see the shine in her eyes and the twinkle that said, wait until we have a moment together. It was time for all of us to start rebuilding our lives.

I wrote a letter home to Josephine and my family. I'm glad I never had to write that letter from the Pacific. Once we were back at the barracks and hangovers wore off, people returned to their senses. We were briefed on the series of events that precipitated the Japanese surrender. Truman authorized the atomic bomb, our secret weapon, to be dropped on the Japanese city of Hiroshima on August 6. Another bomb was dropped on the city of Nagasaki on August 9. Emperor Hirohito surrendered and his War Lords condescended on August 15. The unparalleled destruction of the two bombs that flattened two cities finally did what all the other bombing missions against Japan could not do. Japan surrendered unconditionally.

I went to see the company chaplain two days after the Japanese surrender and told him that Millie and I were getting married. Father McCarthy said that if I got my Baptismal, Communion and Confirmation records sent to him from St. Joseph's parish in New Britain, Connecticut, he could marry us in the church. Millie was a Catholic, and all her records were at the local parish. The Army, however, would not recognize the marriage because it was against regulations for an enlisted man to marry a German woman during occupation. We would have to get married in secret and not live together. Millie could not return with me to the States. So Millie and I decided to wait. I was going to apply to OCS, Officer Candidate School, reenlist once I got back to Connecticut, and ask to be stationed in Germany.

I spent as much time as possible with Millie and her family and then in December 1945, I sailed out of the French port of Marseilles on the USS Mariposa. The Mariposa was a luxury liner before the war, converted by the Navy into a troop transport ship. I was okay until we left the Mediterranean Sea. Then I threw up our victory supper and missed the porthole by three feet. One of the sailors was really disgusted with me. He had just finished swabbing the deck. It was a great meal too, specially prepared for us by an Italian cook, spaghetti and meat balls, a great sauce, and garlic bread.

Though I was happy to be heading home, I missed Millie terribly. Also, I could not get over the sea sickness and I wretched and writhed in my bunk. December storms filled the Straits of Gibraltar, this Atlantic crossing was over a week of rough seas. Sergeant Mack ordered me up.

"No," I said because I could not get up without puking.

Captain Kelly threatened me with court-martial if I did not show up at roll call.

"No Sir," I said since I could not report for roll call if I was too weak to even sit up.

While I lay in my bunk, I read Thomas Merton's Seven Storey Mountain during the Atlantic crossing. It was being passed around the ship, and some of us were trying to make sense of where we'd been and where we were going. On page 248 of Merton's autobiography, I found a passage that resonated with me. "And it would lead me to a land that I could not imagine or understand . . . the land of human nature blinded and fettered by perversity and sin."

I was sick all the way to the States. Once we reached New York Harbor, I somehow commanded my rubber legs to stand. We prepared to disembark. I walked down the ramp out of the ship and looked around. These soldiers that I had spent years with were killing machines, sometimes not much more than animals, and now we were reentering society. I didn't think society was ready for us.

When I arrived at Camp Shanks, it was New Year's Eve. Camp Shanks, near Orangeburg, was outside of NYC. It was a 2000 acre camp, and the staging area for the New York Port of Embarkation and Disembarkation. After we got off the ship, we were brought to a large dining hall and had a welcome home meal, whatever we wanted, cafeteria style. I chose steak, potatoes, spaghetti, fruit cocktail, pie and ice cream. Then I was assigned to a barracks room and was lying in my bunk, digesting everything.

Suddenly, a familiar face appeared before me. "Hey, Johnny, I've been looking all over for you." It was Dominic Criniti, my childhood friend. I jumped up and we hugged and laughed and nearly cried. What a sight he was, a face from the old Italian neighborhood, in fact we'd lived in the same apartment building, ten Italian families in a tenement on Arch Street in New Britain. We were the same age, we'd grown up together, graduated from the same technical school, got drafted at the same time. I saw Dominic occasionally when we were in basic training. We went overseas at the same time, but not in the same outfit. Although we were in different battalions, we both served under General Patton as part of the Third Army, and we both were artillerymen.

I saw Dominic once when we were training overseas in Barry, Wales. How lucky we felt to have found each other, our first night back in the States. We compared notes, swapped battle stories, our hits and near misses, our adventures on European battlefields and how we'd survived. We'd both been assigned to the 105 Howitzer, what a fine piece of artillery. Dominic and I talked all night.

We were both taken to Fort Devon, Massachusetts to be discharged. It was time to go home to see our families in New Britain. I had ninety days to reenlist.

Epilogue

I took off my uniform and hung it at the back of the closet, two days after I returned to Connecticut. Everything had changed. I was disillusioned with the callous, greedy temper of American society when I returned to the States. My contemporaries seemed to have become wealthy on the economy that I helped create while I was fighting in Europe with men dying all around me.

I became unsure of myself. I didn't have a job and couldn't find one. They were given back to the same men who held the jobs before they left for the war. I was a seasoned soldier, but in the work force I was green, fresh out of Goodwin trade school, drafted into the Army before I could land a full time job as an auto mechanic, which was my certification. My father pulled strings and finally got me a factory job. I lived at home. When I finally told my mother that I was going back to Germany, days before the three month re-enlistment period would expire, she nearly broke down, heartsick, wrenched with worry, fearing for my life.

I did not reenlist. Millie married a German engineer and I married a beautiful red-head, an Italian American, mother of my four children. We have ten grandchildren and three great grandchildren. I have twice returned to Europe since the war ended, however, and somehow I still feel more at home there than in the United States.

The two years, nine months that I served in the US Army during World War II were the most exciting and horrible times of my life. Sixty years have passed and I still say, it was the most exciting and horrible time of my life. I even surprise myself at how clearly I remember the events between 1943 and 1946. I kept a diary, which I started in boot camp and wrote in almost daily. From the beginning, I intended to write my war stories. I wrote and received volumes of letters, to and from home. Unfortunately, the diary and letters were lost. I recreated excerpts to the best of my ability, from pages that I'd written, read, and reread before they were lost. I referred not only to books and maps provided to me by the US Army, 90th Division, 343rd battalion, but also consulted with family members, reviewed films, listened to audiobooks, read other soldier's accounts, attended lectures given by war historians, and made visits to a war museum. But mostly I called upon my memory of events, events that have been indelibly etched into my consciousness.

I never attended a 90th Division reunion, and I never saw any of the guys in my gun company, once we returned to the States. As soon as I returned to Connecticut, I kept my promise to Verdel and mailed a registered check to his mother for five thousand dollars. Sergeant James Auwen and I exchanged a few letters. I was able to find one of Auwen's letters, from Camp Lee, Virginia, dated January 17, 1947, written in his school-boyish script. Auwen said, in his understated, unpretentious manner, "Sometimes I wish we were all back together again."